LIBRARY MANUALS

Volume 14

SCHOOL AND COLLEGE LIBRARY PRACTICE

SCHOOL AND COLLEGE LIBRARY PRACTICE

MONICA CANT

LONDON AND NEW YORK

First published 1936 by George Allen & Unwin Ltd
This edition first published in 2022
by Routledge
4 Park Square, Milton Park, Abingdon, Oxon OX14 4RN

and by Routledge
605 Third Avenue, New York, NY 10017

Routledge is an imprint of the Taylor & Francis Group, an informa business

Copyright © 1936 by Taylor & Francis.

All rights reserved. No part of this book may be reprinted or reproduced or utilised in any form or by any electronic, mechanical, or other means, now known or hereafter invented, including photocopying and recording, or in any information storage or retrieval system, without permission in writing from the publishers.

Trademark notice: Product or corporate names may be trademarks or registered trademarks, and are used only for identification and explanation without intent to infringe.

British Library Cataloguing in Publication Data
A catalogue record for this book is available from the British Library

ISBN: 978-1-03-213109-2 (Set)
ISBN: 978-1-00-322771-7 (Set) (ebk)
ISBN: 978-1-03-213597-7 (Volume 14) (hbk)
ISBN: 978-1-03-213598-4 (Volume 14) (pbk)
ISBN: 978-1-00-323004-5 (Volume 14) (ebk)

DOI: 10.4324/9781003230045

Publisher's Note
The publisher has gone to great lengths to ensure the quality of this reprint but points out that some imperfections in the original copies may be apparent.

Disclaimer
The publisher has made every effort to trace copyright holders and would welcome correspondence from those they have been unable to trace.

SCHOOL AND COLLEGE LIBRARY PRACTICE

by

MONICA CANT

*Librarian of the Ladies' College, Cheltenham,
Member of the Committee of Inquiry into
the Provision of Libraries in
Secondary Schools*

LONDON
GEORGE ALLEN & UNWIN LTD
MUSEUM STREET

FIRST PUBLISHED IN 1936

All rights reserved
PRINTED IN GREAT BRITAIN BY
UNWIN BROTHERS LTD., WOKING

GENERAL INTRODUCTION TO THE SERIES

by W. E. DOUBLEDAY, HON. F.L.A.

THIS new Series of Handbooks is intended to supplement the larger Manuals issued by Messrs. Allen & Unwin and the Library Association under the title of *The Library Association Series of Library Manuals.*

There are some aspects of Library work which, although by no means unimportant, are of themselves insufficient to require a full-sized manual, and there are other phases which in a comprehensive textbook of manageable dimensions could be dealt with only in a general way. The Handbooks will adequately cover these subjects and will also treat of certain special topics which hitherto have escaped the attention which they deserve, or which—owing to recent developments—demand reconsideration.

Since Library practice must always be in accordance with the particular requirements of different types and sizes of Libraries, variant methods will be indicated from time to time, and a working basis for individual adoption and comparative study will thus be provided. University, Municipal, School, and Special Libraries —rural as well as urban—will be comprehended within the scope of the Practical Library Handbooks, and in each instance the latest advances will be described.

This smaller Series is issued independently by Messrs. George Allen & Unwin Ltd., and the range is sufficiently wide to make the volumes appeal to Administrators, Librarians, Assistants, and Students who intend to sit at the professional examinations. It is hoped that they will be of great practical assistance for immediate use in enhancing and forwarding still further that improvement in Library service which has been so marked since the passing of the Public Libraries Act of 1919.

PREFACE

As increasing interest is being taken in school libraries, this small handbook is issued in the hope that it may be helpful to those who have charge of such libraries and that, if it should come to the notice of those who are responsible for the administration of schools, it may draw their attention to the considerable amount of detailed work involved in the efficient running of a school library.

Wherever possible, alternative methods have been described so as to meet the needs of the different types of schools and smaller colleges, but these vary so much in their requirements that there may be many problems which have not been covered. I shall, therefore, be glad to hear of points which have been omitted or have been inadequately treated. A certain amount of technical detail has been given so as to make the book more useful to those who are conversant with library organization, together with a number of simple hints which are worth the attention of those to whom they are not already familiar.

To anyone who thinks that the recommendations made seem unduly complicated I can say, with confidence, that in practice they will be found easier than they sound. To any members of the library profession who may glance over the pages that follow I can only appeal, of their charity, to remember that much which they take for granted is not necessarily common knowledge.

My grateful acknowledgments are made to Miss E. S. Fegan, Mr. Arundell Esdaile, Lieut.-Col. J. M. Mitchell, and Mr. W. E. Doubleday for reading the book in manuscript and for their helpful criticisms and suggestions; to a number of Public Librarians and School Librarians for their comments on various matters; also to the schools which allowed me to visit their libraries. I have to thank the Library Association for permission to quote from the Anglo-American cataloguing code and all who have made possible the inclusion of illustrations by lending blocks or consenting to the reproduction of photographs.

MONICA CANT

CONTENTS

CHAPTER		PAGE
	GENERAL INTRODUCTION	7
	PREFACE	9
	LIST OF ILLUSTRATIONS	13
I.	GENERAL REMARKS	15
II.	PLANNING AND EQUIPMENT	25
III.	THE LIBRARY COMMITTEE	34
IV.	BASIC STOCK	43
V.	THE ACQUISITION OF BOOKS	50
VI.	ADDITION TO STOCK AND RECORDS OF STOCK	60
VII.	CLASSIFICATION	72
VIII.	CATALOGUING	88
IX.	ISSUE AND RECALL OF BOOKS	105
X.	BINDING	114
XI.	CO-OPERATION WITHIN THE SCHOOL	122
XII.	SUPPLEMENTARY SERVICES	127
	SELECTED REFERENCES	136
	ADDRESS LIST OF SOCIETIES AND LIBRARIES	140
	INDEX	142

CHRIST'S HOSPITAL GIRLS' SCHOOL, HERTFORD: THE LIBRARY IN 1935
By courtesy of the Architect, Sydney Tatchell, F.R.I.B.A.

LIST OF ILLUSTRATIONS

PLATES

CHRIST'S HOSPITAL GIRLS' SCHOOL, HERTFORD:
THE LIBRARY *Frontispiece*

	FACING PAGE
CARD CABINET WITH INCLINED TRAYS	56

THE LIBRARIES OF—

BERKHAMSTED SCHOOL	32
HEADINGTON SCHOOL FOR GIRLS, OXFORD	64
THE HIGH SCHOOL FOR GIRLS, BRIDLINGTON	64
GRESHAM'S SCHOOL, HOLT	96
PORTSMOUTH HIGH SCHOOL FOR GIRLS, SOUTHSEA	112
ST. PAUL'S SCHOOL, WEST KENSINGTON	120
NORWICH TRAINING COLLEGE	128

FIGURES IN TEXT

	PAGE
GUIDE CARDS FOR SUGGESTION FILE	53
RECORD CARDS FOR PERIODICALS	58
ACCESSION REGISTER	62
SHELF-LIST	65
AUTHOR CATALOGUE CARD	92

14   SCHOOL & COLLEGE LIBRARY PRACTICE

	PAGE
SUBJECT CATALOGUE CARD	99
ANALYTICAL SUBJECT CARD	102
ISSUE CARD	107
BORROWER'S SLIP	108
LIBRARY HUNT FORMS	134

SCHOOL AND COLLEGE LIBRARY PRACTICE

CHAPTER I

GENERAL REMARKS

ONE of the most, if not the most, delightful points about any kind of work connected with libraries is the fascination it exercises over the worker. Very often conditions may be hard, hours long, pay small, and results not easily measurable, but those who once begin generally grow more and more interested. The recently issued report[1] of the Committee set up by the Carnegie United Kingdom Trust on Secondary School Libraries gives the conclusions reached after a lengthy and searching inquiry into the present state and future possibilities of school libraries in this country. Its recommendations should be closely studied by anyone who is interested in the subject. As, however, the Committee felt that detailed descriptions of practical routine matters did not come within their terms of reference, a manual for the school librarian may have its uses. Such a manual may even be of service in the libraries of the smaller and non-university colleges.

[1] See Selected References.

BASIC PRINCIPLES

The library in a school or college is what has been called a "one-purpose" library, for it serves a closely knit community whose work lies along fairly well-defined lines. It is, therefore, able to exclude all material that is either unnecessary or unsuitable to the furtherance of its particular aim. Secondly, it is essentially a working collection of good modern editions, though luxuries such as items of historical interest or intrinsic value may be very welcome gifts. Thirdly, it is not an independent institution but owes its existence to the school or college of whose machinery it forms a part. Finally, the library combines reference and lending functions, all books on the shelves being available for consultation and all but a few of encyclopaedic character being available for borrowing. In this respect the use of the term "Reference Library" in school parlance is unfortunate. It is generally applied to the school library proper to distinguish it from fiction and other subsidiary libraries, but as the majority of the books are not really reference books, it seems a pity to use the misnomer; to say "the Library" is truer and more dignified.

THE LIBRARY AS A UNITY

If, as often happens, there are several different libraries scattered about the school, it is highly desirable that they should be co-ordinated so that some one person is responsible for the library as a whole, even if different sections are under the immediate charge of other people. It is much better if all the books can be brought together in the library room, except possibly popular fiction and such books as laboratory manuals which are constantly referred to during lessons. The library should represent learning as a unity and should act as a counterweight to the ever-increasing tendency to early specialization. As universities find that their departmental libraries are apt to get out of hand, so schools should take warning against scattering their much smaller resources.

FINANCE

Discussion of matters of policy would be out of place in a handbook of this sort except in so far as they affect the practical side. One such matter is the requisite amount of money. Where no library exists a fairly substantial outlay will be necessary which can be spread over two or three years. Having been started, the library can only progress by being assured of an annual income. *The Report of the Carnegie Committee on Secondary School Libraries* gives three shillings per head as an adequate minimum for a school of three hundred pupils, allowing rather more proportionately for smaller schools and less for larger schools.

A specific sum definitely allocated for library purposes by the Governing Body is the most effective form of income, the amount naturally being subject to revision from time to time. It is advisable that unexpended balances should be permitted to be carried forward as otherwise there may be a tendency to spend up to the hilt in order not to lose the money. Some schools make a charge for the library in the accounts of pupils or levy a small subscription, but these methods are often not applicable and are not altogether satisfactory, though it may be necessary to resort to them as a supplementary source of income.

THE SCHOOL LIBRARIAN

Another very practical matter is that of the school librarian. It is now generally recognized that it is necessary to secure your librarian before you can hope to have a library, but schools frequently appear to think that the order can be reversed. Consequently one sometimes comes across instances of waste that could have been avoided by beginning on the right lines. As the library has grown, the existing arrangement has broken down and reorganization become necessary, a state of affairs that may even be repeated within a few years. There are occasions when complete reorganization is called for, but successive new starts can only be regarded as setbacks. Continuity is difficult to maintain in a school library owing to the more or less frequent change of librarian, but if the arrangements for the running of the library are drawn up in the first instance by someone acquainted with library methods as well as with the school's requirements, together with a set of explanations and instructions which can be handed on from one librarian to another, it should be possible to carry the system steadily on with only minor adjustments to meet new needs.

The memoranda should state clearly the procedure that is followed and the appropriate seasons for carrying out recurring duties. The value of such memoranda to a successor is very great; if, at some time, it should be decided that alteration is desirable it will have the advantage of being a considered change and not one that has come about through ignorance of previous practice. Even the librarian who has compiled the notes will find that an occasional glance through them will often save sins of omission. Needless to say that the notes must be kept up to date or they will nullify their own object. The librarian will be well advised to keep a loose-leaf address book with headings such as Booksellers, Binders, Library Supply Firms; also a record of supplies ordered with full particulars so that it is easy to turn up details when a further supply is required.

LIBRARY TRAINING AND MEMBERSHIP OF THE LIBRARY ASSOCIATION

If there is any difficulty in finding someone competent to undertake the initial organization of the library, the school should communicate with the local Public Librarian or with the Library Association, Chaucer House, Malet Place, London, W.C.1, or with the School of Librarianship, University College, Gower Street, London, W.C.1.

It is very desirable that short courses of training in library methods should be organized for members of school staffs who are in charge of school libraries. The report of the Carnegie Committee[1] urges the provision of vacation courses by Government Education Departments acting in consultation with the Library Association and the Scottish Library Association. These Library Associations are in a position to advise on the syllabus for such courses and to recommend persons fully qualified to give instruction on technical matters.

An experimental course of a week has already been held at Oxford by the Board of Education. Not very much can be done in a week, but a three-week course should give a really useful insight into most of the essentials and those attending should thereby be saved much perplexity and waste of time and expenditure. The value of such a course would consist not only in the information obtained from lectures and demonstrations, but also in the opportunities that would be available for the discussion of problems with other school librarians.

More extended training for those who desire it is available at the School of Librarianship, but the full year's training required of a graduate is more than is warranted by the position of a part-time librarian in

[1] See Selected References.

most schools. Full-time school librarians in this country are rare, though in the United States they form a strong section of the library profession and have done much to make the library the focus of school education.

There is not at present any body which regularly arranges meetings and conferences of school librarians as such. Authorities for Higher Education might with advantage undertake this for their own areas, but the appropriate central body is the Library Association. By joining it, school librarians would be brought into contact with other librarians with whom discussions would be very helpful. The Association comprises librarians of all types and already many university librarians are members. It is the one body which unites library workers and furthers their interests in every way possible. Attendance at the Annual Conference and Exhibition of Library Appliances is a fruitful source of new ideas. To those who wish to keep abreast of the latest developments, it is an advantage to be able to purchase the Association's publications at the special rate for members.

The annual subscription of £2 2s. is higher than most school librarians feel justified in paying, but a scheme for the reorganization of grades of membership is under consideration, and it is much to be hoped that it may be found possible to introduce a lower rate of subscription for part-time librarians.

PUBLIC LIBRARY CO-OPERATION

A number of municipal Public Libraries afford facilities to schools, such as admitting pupils as borrowers on the recommendation of the head teacher, allowing books to be kept out over an extended period, arranging for pupils to work in the reference library, obtaining books from other libraries, giving library talks, and explaining the use of reference books. When the Public Library is near the school every advantage should be taken of the privileges offered. If pupils during their school years are trained in the use of the Public Library, they will be much more likely to continue to take out books after they have left. If this training is not possible, the school might arrange for leaving-pupils to make a conducted tour of the Public Library, at the end of which they would be handed application forms for borrowers' tickets.

Many elementary and some secondary schools are supplied with collections of books for general reading by both municipal and county libraries. These are very valuable supplements to the school book stock but do not take the place of the school's own library. Unless the loan collection is entirely fiction, it will be most satisfactory if it can be kept in the same room as the school collection, thus forming a complete library.

County libraries, owing to their close connection with schools and the fact that their stock is almost entirely available for lending, usually make no charge, or only charge for return carriage on books lent; in towns the provision of books to schools is usually dependent on some financial arrangement between the Education and Library Committees. The collections supplied are generally changed at intervals, though a certain number of volumes may be deposited permanently. Experiments in the establishment of branches of the Public Library in schools have been made in Edinburgh, Manchester, and Leicester. Fuller accounts will be found in *Books in Public Elementary Schools*[1] and in the *Report on Secondary School Libraries*.[2] A description of the organization of school collections supplied by Public Libraries will be found in *A Manual of Children's Libraries*,[3] by W. C. Berwick Sayers.

In some localities, schools are given representation on the Public Library Committee by the co-option of one of the teachers. This is a useful link which might with mutual advantage be adopted more generally.

Even if there is no formal connection with the Public Library, school librarians can benefit by keeping in close touch with the municipal or county library for the area. They should make themselves personally known to the librarian, study the arrangement of the library and acquaint themselves with its stock. They will then be able to draw profitably on its resources. They will probably find that they will be allowed to

---

[1] See Selected References.   [2] Ibid.   [3] Ibid.

have not only books from the lending department, but even some from the reference department for use in the school library on the understanding that these will be returned promptly if required. Additional reference books can be obtained through the Public Library from the National Central Library (see p. 127). Also, by examining a book at the Public Library, it is often possible to decide whether it should be added to the school library. School librarians are, unfortunately, rarely in a position to render return courtesy, though when this is possible they will naturally be glad to do so. This consideration need not deter them from the use of the Public Library, for it is a public institution maintained out of the rates to which the school is a contributor. They should, however, realize that the Public Library has many claims to meet, and be careful to make only reasonable requests.

STANDING COMMITTEE ON SCHOOL LIBRARIES

The Secondary School Libraries Committee in their report to the Carnegie Trustees recommend that a standing committee should be set up to whom reference could be made on matters pertaining to school libraries. The Standing Committee would, almost certainly, be prepared to give advice on book selection and to furnish the addresses of firms from whom library supplies and materials for home binding could be obtained, besides promoting the general advancement of school library provision and organization.

CHAPTER II

PLANNING AND EQUIPMENT

IF, as is most likely, an existing room is to be used for the library, much can be done by careful planning of the furniture to make the best use of the space. If a room is being built, it is most important to determine dimensions from within outwards. The librarian should first be consulted as to his requirements and the architect then asked to make his plan. As a check on the area requisite, an allowance of 30 to 35, or preferably 35 to 40, square feet per reader may be taken as a basis; this will provide for gangways and space for the shelving of an adequate number of books. The shelving should be kept as low as possible, particularly any double-sided cases standing out in the room. The spaces between windows should take bookcases of standard size and, wherever possible, wall space should be available for shelving. In deciding on the arrangement of the interior, it is easy to make a scale drawing on squared paper and, by using small pieces of paper to represent bookcases and tables, to experiment on the layout. A very detailed discussion on planning is given in Chapter IX of *The Library in the School*,[1] by L. F. Fargo.

[1] See Selected References.

LIBRARIAN'S OFFICE

The library is one of the parts of the school that can most easily be shown to visitors and it should be presentable at all times. This desirable state of affairs will be greatly facilitated by the provision of a small adjoining room which the librarian can use as an office and workroom. Alternatively, a portion of the library might be partitioned off by standing bookcases. In the librarian's office, books in course of being catalogued or awaiting rebinding can be left without danger of being disturbed, library supplies stored, minor repairs executed, and typewriting done. Necessary fitments are running water, a gas-ring, a work-bench, cupboards large enough to take unfolded sheets of card and mounting paper, a couple of chairs, and some shelving.

DISCUSSION ROOM

A discussion room, possibly combined with a recreational reading-room, also adjoining the library, would complete the provision. Modern novels and other works that are only issued at stated times could be kept in cases closed by a grill or pull-down shutters. The room need not be large but, if it can be provided, readers in the library proper need not be disturbed when a teacher wishes to demonstrate to a group the materials available on the topic in hand, or when small groups of pupils have work to do which they need to talk over amongst themselves. Books could be brought through from the library and left there as long as required and need not be entered in the issue register as they would have to be if sent to a classroom. Moreover, they would be available for pupils from several classes. The discussion room could also be used by individual readers at such times as a class lesson on the use of the library was being given. While many schools have not, as yet, even one room solely devoted to library purposes, it may seem a counsel of perfection to advocate the provision of a second room, but schools which wish to plan for the future should at least consider its advantages.

LIGHTING

Good lighting, both natural and artificial, is all-important in a library. The correct relationship between the height of the windows and the width of the room, and the placing of reading-tables to avoid both glare and cross-shadows, have to be considered. Books absorb a great deal of light, so that the reflecting value of bare wall spaces should be enhanced as much as possible. For instance, primrose yellow has nearly twice the reflecting power of light sage green or pale grey. The permanence of the wall surface and the ease with which it can be cleaned also need to be taken into account. Redecoration is a trying as well as a costly business, and even a thin film of dust greatly reduces reflecting power. Windows should be easy to clean, for much light may be lost by passing through dirty glass. The most pleasing and generally satisfactory form of artificial lighting is that diffused from built-in light sources; if there are alcoves they will need to be individually lit.

HEATING

The maintenance of the right temperature in the library will make a great difference to the comfort of the readers and its adequate ventilation will help the output of good work. The heating of the library will probably be on the system operating throughout the school and the librarian will have little to do except to co-operate with the engineer by exercising discretion in the opening of windows. Heating systems are highly technical and even controversial matters; it may, however, be remarked that with any hot-water system care should be taken to secure complete insulation of any connecting pipes that pass near bookcases or the covers of the books will curl outwards. Those who wish to make a detailed study of heating and lighting are referred to *Library Buildings*,[1] edited by R. D. Hilton Smith.

FLOOR COVERING

Solid oak-block flooring is as good as anything; it is perhaps more noisy than some other materials, but the squeaking and scratching of chairs being pulled in and out can be greatly reduced by the use of "domes

[1] See Selected References.

of silence." Sound-absorbing materials which can be recommended are compressed cork tiles and the Dunlop rubber flooring. The cork tiles will take a fair polish and can easily be renewed. The Dunlop flooring is obtainable in attractive shades, and if a colour mottled with black is chosen, ink marks will not be noticeable. It is, however, a new material that has not yet been fully proven as to wearing qualities. Whatever material is chosen, it should be easy to clean and pleasing to look upon, so that it will not need relieving by rugs which, however much they may add to the scheme of decoration, do make a certain amount of "fluff" and are apt to be dangerous on a polished floor.

CLEANING

The general cleaning of the library is usually done with that of the rest of the school buildings, but the cleaning of the books is more directly the concern of the librarian. A school cleaner let loose on the shelves may work havoc with the order of the books. An occasional thorough cleaning, removing all books, with an electric vacuum apparatus under the librarian's supervision will usually suffice. If the cleaning is not supervised, a complete shelf-check will be necessary after it to restore the books to their correct places.

SHELVING

For bookcases and other fittings most schools will choose wood in preference to steel as it is much more harmonious, even if more expensive. It cannot be too strongly emphasized that all library equipment should be as interchangeable as possible; shelf units all of the same length, shelves movable, card and filing cabinets of standard size. In the newer designs for bookcases the bottom shelf is tilted upward and outward so that the titles of the books can be more easily seen, and the front edges of the shelves are grooved to take the shelf labels (see p. 87). The regulation length for a shelf is 3 feet. It is usual to calculate nine volumes to a foot, but eight volumes is a better figure to take where the majority of the books are larger than ordinary novels. The shelves may be 8 to 9 inches wide for all ordinary books. One or two deeper cases for the art section, encyclopaedias, and other large books may have shelves as wide as 14 inches. Fixed vertical supports midway in each tier will help to keep these heavy books upright. It may happen that only some of the shelves in a wide case are needed for oversize books; if the other shelves are used for smaller books, these can be kept from slipping to the back by screwing a block of wood to each upright and glueing a lath to the blocks. The contrivance can quickly be removed when the library acquires more large books.

The height of wall cases should not exceed 6 feet 6 inches over all. This allows for six shelf spaces of 10 to 11 inches in the clear between the shelves, a cornice, and a deep base which makes the books on the bottom shelves more accessible and helps to keep dust from them. If many of the younger children use the library, 5 feet 6 inches (5 shelf spaces) would be better. Double-sided projecting or free-standing cases are sometimes the same height as the wall cases, but this is not desirable. If they are kept low (four shelf spaces) the room has a much pleasanter and more open appearance.

TABLES AND CHAIRS

The presentation of tables and chairs by former pupils is a very suitable way of expressing their regard for their old school. Tables should be absolutely rigid, and be independent structurally of any bar provided for a foot-rest. To prevent ink stains from sinking into the wood, the tops may be coated with eggshell varnish in a flat finish, or with a cellulose finish like that used on the bodywork of cars. The cellulose finish is excellent when newly done, but there seems to be some doubt whether it will last many years. With either of these, ink remains on the surface and can be wiped off if not allowed to stand too long. There is a new kind of linoleum now on the market which is almost impervious to ink; this should be a suitable covering for table tops. Tables should not seat more than six persons and ample gangway space (not less than 3 feet) should be allowed for the pushing back of chairs. Chairs need to be of the right height in relation to the tables. A few free-standing chairs which allow a more reclining position, one or two low window-seats, a round table or single reading-desk in an angle, help to break the formality of the room and make a pleasing contrast to the rectangular lines of the rest of the furniture.

MISCELLANEOUS EQUIPMENT

Other essentials of equipment are a desk for the librarian; something of the flat-topped writing-desk variety with kneehole and drawers is all that is required. At least one drawer should be provided with lock and key for the safe keeping of stamps and petty cash. The desk should be placed at a strategic point where incomings and outgoings can be kept under observation. Near the desk should be the catalogue cabinet, below which may be shallow shelves for current magazines, or cupboards with sliding doors for filing back numbers. The modern cabinets with inclined trays are a great improvement on the older makes. The cards automatically arrange themselves in a sloping position which makes them easy to consult, while the rod which runs through the cards to secure them only needs a lift of the finger to release it.

A display rack, made of two or three troughs one above the other, is very useful for showing new books, for special displays on subjects of interest, or for books which are placed on the reserve list (see p. 111). A stand having a single book trough surmounted by a canvas-covered slope large enough to take illustrated papers or newspaper cuttings of a column in length,

BERKHAMSTED SCHOOL: THE LIBRARY IN 1933
By courtesy of P. A. Buchanan & Co., Ltd.

would allow a combined display of books and sheet material, and would be useful for stimulating interest in current events. A stand for atlases, which may be built-in, is another desirable piece of furniture. Half a dozen shelves, each to take one or two books lying flat, surmounted by a slightly sloping desk top with a raised bevel at the front edge on which the volumes may be consulted, will encourage reference to the books by making them easier to use.

CHAPTER III

THE LIBRARY COMMITTEE

MANY schools do not have a committee to determine the policy of the library and administer its funds, this work resting with the Head and the librarian, who, no doubt, confer with specialists on the choice of books. In matters of school policy and discipline the Head must always decide, but there are other matters that can be dealt with by a committee. The smaller school libraries may not need the machinery of a committee, but it is an advantage to have a definite body of people who have certain responsibilities in connection with the library; it makes for spreading interest in the library through the school and ensures that the knowledge and experience of the staff are regularly drawn upon.

FUNCTIONS OF THE LIBRARY COMMITTEE

The chief functions of the Library Committee are:—
(1) To apportion the library budget.
(2) To make a balanced selection of books and periodicals.
(3) To determine regulations for the use of the library.
(4) To make suggestions for increasing its usefulness.
(5) To receive the annual report of the librarian.

It is not uncommon to find committees whose chief business is to assist and relieve the librarian in routine duties, but their main function should be book selection. Student help can be provided by the appointment of selected pupils as library prefects or assistant librarians, and they may be given representation on the committee.

CONSTITUTION OF THE LIBRARY COMMITTEE

School library committees may be composed, either by appointment or election, of members of staff either with or without representatives of the senior pupils, the Head being an *ex-officio* member. It is very valuable if a member of the Governing Body can be induced to accept the office of chairman. A meeting once a term will usually be found sufficient if discretionary powers are granted to the librarian to purchase books required to meet an urgent need or obtainable at special prices, subject to the purchase being reported at the next meeting.

ANNUAL BUDGET

It is probably most usual and certainly most satisfactory for the school stationery department to provide such supplies as library forms, catalogue cards, and mending materials, though occasionally these are bought by the library. As for additional bookcases, cabinets, and so on, these are obviously part of the school furnishing and, unless there is a specially increased grant to cover them, it would be unreasonable to charge them to the library fund.

The library expenditure, therefore, will fall under the heads:—

(1) New books (i.e. new to the library whether bought new or secondhand).
(2) Replacements.
(3) Periodicals and subscriptions.
(4) Binding.
(5) Emergency fund.

In an established library it will be found that, barring exceptional circumstances, expenditure varies little from year to year, and an analysis of the previous year's expenditure with slight modifications will serve as the budget. The principal item is new books and, if the amount required on the other items is ascertained, the rest of the money will be available for additions. The last four items will accordingly be taken first. Replacements will not figure in the budget of a newly organized library, but in any established library a small sum should be set aside for the librarian to spend without reference to the committee in replacing worn-out or out-of-date copies of standard works; otherwise a sort of dry rot will set in and the quality of the book stock gradually deteriorate. The purchase of duplicate copies should generally be brought before the committee.

Most schools cannot afford to spend much on periodicals and subscriptions to societies, but one of the principal dailies, *The Times Literary Supplement*, and one or two good reviews, such as *Greece and Rome* and the *Geographical Magazine*, should be provided. *L'Illustration*, though expensive, is of real value, as it can be used in many ways, and the illustrations in its special numbers are superb. Subscriptions to the English and Historical Associations, the British Drama League, and to the local archaeological society are very desirable. Lighter magazines will probably be provided only where there is a magazine club with a small subscription, or where individual pupils who take a magazine regularly are willing to lend the numbers for a period.

The committee should allocate the amount that can be spent on binding and repairing, and leave the librarian to lay it out to the best advantage.

A small sum set aside as an emergency fund for unforeseen expenses will prevent any difficulty over paying for books which may not be delivered, owing to reprinting or other causes, for some time after they have been ordered.

CONSIDERATION OF NEW BOOKS

The other items having been disposed of, the amount available for new books can be ascertained and this amount divided roughly into the sums which can be spent at each meeting; not necessarily into equal parts as the heaviest book outlay is most advantageously made at the principal meeting at the beginning, or in preparation for the beginning, of the school year. The list of books proposed for addition, grouped by subjects (see p. 52), should be circulated to the members with the agenda for the meeting. Sometimes a general vote is taken on each book, but when this is done, specialist views are apt to be passed over. It is, therefore, a good plan for the chairman to give the representative of each subject an opportunity to indicate which books are more particularly required, and for what purpose; then when these have been voted upon, to take the rest of the list item by item. If, as may happen by this method, books required for examination work tend to crowd out books of general interest, the balance can be restored by gathering into a separate section those books that do not clearly belong to any one subject group and setting aside a suitable proportion of income for their purchase. A method which allows for variation in the needs of the different subjects is distinctly preferable to allocating a fixed sum to each subject. New needs created by a change in the curriculum can be catered for, and there is no inducement to spend money merely because it has been assigned. A subject that has been generously treated at one meeting will usually make a modest claim at the next, and even if the sense of give and take is not thus far developed, the representatives of the other subjects will see that it does not get more than its due.

An alternative method of book selection, which

renders a committee unnecessary, is described in the *Report of the Secondary School Libraries Committee*.[1] Briefly, it is to allocate the amounts up to which each specialist responsible for a subject may select books, reserving a certain amount for the librarian to spend on books of general interest.

LIBRARY REGULATIONS

The rules should be neither many nor complicated, but until they are decided the most suitable methods of administration cannot be determined, for these should interact. For instance, the method chosen for registering issues (see Chapter IX) will depend on whether or no there is a time limit for books borrowed. Each school will make such regulations as will best fit its own purposes; the following are suggested as points which might be considered:—

(1) Use of the library to be permitted to all pupils, or to be restricted, more particularly for purposes of study, to those from senior classes or those specially recommended.
(2) Hours open for reading and borrowing. It should be possible for borrowers to change their books whenever they are free to come to the library.
(3) Books not to be marked in any way.
(4) Dictionaries, atlases, and other permanent refer-

[1] See Selected References.

ence books to be confined to the library, also any books whilst on the reserve list (see p. 111).

(5) Every book or paper taken out of the library to be entered (see Chapter IX).

(6) Number of volumes that may be borrowed. If a generous limit is fixed, say five volumes, and exceptions made for special cases, no hardship will be occasioned and there will be a check on the book vamp who takes books but does not use them.

(7) Time limit for borrowing. Preferably no fixed limit, but provision made for recall after reasonable period if required by another reader.

(8) Returned books not to be put on the shelves, but in a place appointed. Books used in the library may be put back in their places or preferably left on the tables for student assistants to replace.

(9) All books to be recalled before the end of term.

(10) Holidays books. Number allowed. All to be returned at the beginning of term.

(11) Penalties. For loss or damage; for taking out a book without entering it; for non-return of a book when recalled. Fines for non-return are objectionable, they might perhaps be imposed only if a second application has to be made. Serious offences may call for suspension of library privileges.

Silence should be maintained in the library as far as possible, but pupils will readily appreciate this, and it is hardly necessary to make it a clause in the regulations. In some school libraries the use of ink is prohibited; this detracts from the general usefulness of the library, and ink should certainly be allowed at some tables if not all. Suggestions are made in Chapter II for the protection of tables against damage by ink.

MINUTES AND ANNUAL REPORT

A minute book for entering the proceedings of the committee will be required. Minutes need not be lengthy, but should state clearly proposals made and decisions reached. Red ink headings in the margin are an aid to reference. Such matters as members present, balance in hand at the date of the meeting, names of donors, periodicals to be taken or discontinued, number of volumes and their cost sanctioned for purchase, will appear in the minutes as regular items. A list of the titles passed will scarcely be necessary if the librarian's marked copy of the book list is filed (see p. 53).

A committee that is really interested in the progress of the library will be glad to have a short review of the year's work presented at its principal meeting. The librarian will naturally take the opportunity to comment on any features particularly noteworthy. Whether detailed statistics should be included will depend on the wishes of the committee, but, generally speaking, the librarian is better employed in administering the library than in preparing elaborate tables of figures. Such figures as are given should lend themselves to constructive interpretation, and if they are circulated with the agenda, time will be saved at the meeting. The full details of the report will be permanently recorded in the minute book.

The most necessary statistics are those relating to finance and stock. A statement of income and expenditure should be given with the expenditure analysed under the heads suggested on p. 36 in the section "Annual Budget." When periodicals are obtained from an agent who also supplies books the rendering of separate invoices will facilitate the preparation of this part of the report. If the accounts are paid and filed by the secretary's office, the librarian will need to make notes of the amounts under the appropriate headings before sending bills up for payment.

The statistics of stock should include the number of volumes in the library and the number of additions and withdrawals during the year which can be analysed, if desired, under main subjects. These particulars can be obtained from the accession and withdrawal registers (see p. 61). Statistics of issues have not the same importance in a school as in a public library, but they may be useful as a proof of the value of the library.

CHAPTER IV

BASIC STOCK

For the school or college which decides to build up a library or which wants to strengthen an existing stock, there are various lists and bibliographies available; some of the most useful publications for this purpose are given at the end of the chapter.

OVERHAUL OF EXISTING STOCK

The first step in making a revision of stock is to take a survey of the books the library already has. They should be gathered together, sorted into main subjects, and with the help of the teachers who have charge of subjects, divided into useful, doubtful, and not-wanted groups. The librarian should bear in mind that a book condemned by a specialist may possibly be useful to other people, and that specialists, who do not always agree, may come and go. Therefore if any uncertainty is felt about some of the condemned volumes it will be advisable to put them, at any rate for the time being, with those classed as doubtful. The useful books will form the nucleus of the library, and can be brought into stock and prepared for issue (see Chapter VI). The doubtful books may be put aside till experience shows whether they are worth including in the library, or whether it is possible to buy better books to take their place. If some of the doubtful books are asked for, they should be added to the library records before being circulated. It is a mistake to put books into the library just because the shelves look rather naked at first; unwanted books are worse than useless because they detract from the appeal of the library and readers are apt to assume that they represent the general level of the stock.

BUILDING UP THE COLLECTION

Having put his possessions in order, the librarian will be in a position to collect suggestions of books wanted. The best method is to enter each suggestion, whether received from members of the staff or obtained from the lists of books used as guides, on a separate card or slip. The particulars that will be required (see p. 51) must be noted on each. The cards should be sorted under subjects; some titles will be selected for immediate purchase and the cards for the others reserved for later consideration. A good outline of the kinds of books most needed is given in the *Memorandum on Libraries in Secondary Schools*,[1] but it is not necessary to attempt to carry out immediately all the recommendations made there. It would be a pity to overload the library at the beginning with learned works. A fair proportion of attractive books of general interest will be a means of drawing borrowers to the library; later on the collection may be strengthened in

[1] See Selected References.

the directions found to be needed. In the purchase of reference books in particular, the librarian should be content to go slowly. There are some books which the library must have, but in many instances a good deal of reconnoitring will have to precede the choice even of standard works recommended in authoritative lists. Reference books are expensive, and though there should be no hesitation in buying a costly work when it will be so useful that the library cannot afford to be without it, other books may be considered too expensive to justify their addition to a small collection. When the absolutely essential books have been bought, it is probably best to build up the library subject by subject, having due regard to the urgency of curriculum requirements.

OCCASIONS FOR CAUTION

The librarian should be on the look-out for the tendency, sometimes manifested by teachers keen on their subject, to ask for books that are more suited to a university than a school library. Even if they justify the request by saying that the book in question is the only one on that particular aspect, the librarian should remember that there is the possibility of other books being published and should see if meanwhile the book can be obtained from some other library (see p. 127). Works hawked round for which orders are solicited and jobbed-off books of all kinds are justifiably suspect. The buying of long complete sets and series may often be uneconomic, for the volumes are not always of equal quality and some of them may be outside the school range. The buying of such sets in bulk may absorb money that could be laid out to better purpose. There is, as a rule, no real difficulty in buying a few volumes at a time.

DISCRETIONARY POWERS OF LIBRARIAN

In the selection of books for the basic stock, as in the ordinary process of book selection, the lists will be submitted to the Library Committee, but rather more discretion should be allowed the librarian to acquire books when and as opportunity occurs. Useful books may be found cheap at secondhand booksellers and in the stores of the big circulating libraries (see p. 55). These should be snapped up without waiting for a committee meeting.

As the books are received, they will be put through the usual processes of addition to the library (see Chapter VI) and take their places on the shelves. When the first selection of books in all the main subjects has been bought, the librarian will find the shelf-list (see p. 64) an invaluable guide in showing where the library is weak and thus indicating gaps which need to be filled.

Gifts may be made a very useful source of increase, but if an appeal is issued in the School Magazine indication of the kind of books desired should be given, and it should be made quite clear that the librarian should be consulted before any books are sent.

AIDS TO BOOK SELECTION

NOTE.—When the name of a publisher is given, the book may be obtained through any bookseller; for the others, direct application should be made to the society concerned. For the addresses of societies, see Address List.

BIBLIOGRAPHIES: GENERAL

JOURNAL OF EDUCATION. The issues for January 1933 to May 1934 contain articles on the various sections of a school library with valuable lists of books. Obtainable from any newsagent. 8d. each.

LIBRARY ASSOCIATION. Books for youth: a classified and annotated guide; ed. by W. C. Berwick Sayers. New ed. [of the work formerly entitled Books to read]. 1936. 10s. To members 9s.

    A most useful list of interesting books on all subjects; it also includes fiction. Every school library should possess a copy.

—— Reference books: a classified and annotated guide to the principal works of reference, and Supplement; compiled by J. Minto, 1929–31. £1 1s. and 10s. 6d. School librarians who do not feel justified in purchasing this can consult it at any good Public Library.

LONDON COUNTY COUNCIL. Catalogue of the Education Library. 1935. 5s. A classified and annotated catalogue, with detailed subject index, of the London County Council's circulating library for teachers.

NATIONAL BOOK COUNCIL. Book lists prepared by authorities on their subjects are issued to associate members. Some but not all are useful to schools. Subscription 7s. 6d.

ROBERTSON, J. M., ed. Courses of study. 3rd ed. 1932. Watts. 5s.

Six to sixteen, what they read: the catalogue of the circulating library of the Children's Book Club, compiled by Mrs. Charles Bridge. 2nd ed. 1934. 2s. 6d. A useful list of selected titles, specially for younger readers. Has both fiction and subject sections; that on historical fiction is particularly good. Titles are marked to indicate the approximate ages for which they are suitable.

BIBLIOGRAPHIES: SPECIAL

BRITISH DRAMA LEAGUE. The Player's library II. 1934. 2s. 6d.

DYMOND, D. Handbook for history teachers. 4th ed. in prep. Methuen.

ENGLISH ASSOCIATION. A Reference library of English language and literature. 2nd ed. 1927. 1s.

FORSAITH, D. M. Handbook for geography teachers. 1932. Methuen. 4s.

HISTORICAL ASSOCIATION. Annual bulletin of historical literature. Bell. 1s. 6d.*Free to members.

—— Leaflets. Many of these contain bibliographies; the most useful are:—

Historical novels, by C. H. Firth. No. 51. 1925.

List of books in English on ancient history for the use of teachers in schools, by N. H. Baynes. No. 84. 1931. Bell. 1s. each.

INCORPORATED ASSOCIATION OF ASSISTANT MASTERS. Memorandum on the teaching of English. 1927. 3s. 6d.

—— Memorandum on the teaching of geography. 1935. Philip. 7s. 6d.

MATHEMATICAL ASSOCIATION. List of books for school libraries. 1926. Bell. 1s.

POWER, E. Bibliography for school teachers of history. 2nd ed. 1921. Methuen. 1s. 6d.

SCIENCE MASTERS' ASSOCIATION and THE ASSOCIATION OF WOMEN SCIENCE TEACHERS. Books suitable for school science libraries. New ed. 1935. 1s.

SOCIETIES FOR THE PROMOTION OF HELLENIC AND ROMAN STUDIES. The Claim of antiquity: an annotated list of books. 4th ed. 1935. Oxford University Press. 1s.

BASIC STOCK

LISTS OF PRICES

Reference catalogue of current literature. Every four years. Whitaker. £4. In advance £3.

English catalogue of books. Annually. Publishers' Circular Ltd. 15s. An alphabetical list.

Whitaker's cumulative book list. Quarterly parts cumulated into an annual volume. Whitaker. £1 5s. Annual volume separately, 15s. Classified and alphabetical lists.

Books of the month. Monthly. Simpkin Marshall. Supplied free by some booksellers. A selected list.

Current literature. Monthly. Whitaker. 4d.

Publishers' catalogues and lists of new publications. Usually supplied on request.

PERIODICALS USEFUL FOR REVIEWS OF BOOKS

The following may be obtained from any newsagent, the journals of societies excepted.

Classical Review. Monthly. 2s.
Contemporary Review. Monthly. 3s. 6d.
The Economist. Weekly. 1s.
Geography, the journal of the Geographical Association. Quarterly. 10s. a year.
Greece and Rome. Three issues a year. 3s.
History, the journal of the Historical Association. Quarterly. 10s. a year.
The Listener. Weekly. 3d.
The London Mercury. Monthly. 1s.
Music and Letters. Quarterly. 5s.
Nature. Weekly. 1s.
The New Statesman. Weekly. 6d.
The Observer. Weekly. 2d.
The Studio. Monthly. 2s.
The Times Literary Supplement. Weekly. 3d.
Young Opinion, the Journal of the Junior Book Club. Three issues a year. 6d.

CHAPTER V

THE ACQUISITION OF BOOKS

BOTH the library committee and the librarian have a part to play in the acquisition of books. Chapter III was concerned with the procedure of the committee; this chapter concerns the librarian's share in book selection and ordering. The subject has been treated in some detail because the amount of time and work involved in discriminating book buying is not always realized.

PREPARATION OF BOOK-LISTS

Book-lists, for the consideration of the Head or of the Library Committee, should combine suggestions from specialists, from the librarian, and from other members of the school, whether staff or pupils. The librarian should hold a watching brief to see that obvious gaps are filled, that successive volumes of works in course of publication are bought, and that such general works—encyclopaedias, year-books, and bibliographical aids—as the library needs, are added. The only really satisfactory way to keep notes of books likely to be useful is to enter each item on a separate card or slip of the standard size of 5 by 3 inches, as these can be sorted and combined as required. When reading reviews or browsing in book shops or other libraries, it is advisable to note down not only author and title, but also publisher, month and year of publication, price, and source of suggestion. These details can be jotted down in a few moments, but if not secured may be difficult to trace afterwards. The name of the publisher is often a guide to the quality of a book, and the exact date of publication is a help in determining how soon it is likely to be available at a reduced price (see p. 55). The cards, kept in a tray or drawer, form a suggestion file. A suggestion book, kept where it is easily available, offers readers a simple way of proposing books. The entries in the suggestion book will from time to time need transferring to cards and incorporating in the suggestion file. It does not do to rely entirely on chance suggestions; a balanced selection is probably best assured if the librarian, well in advance of a meeting, asks teachers in charge of subjects to submit lists of their requirements. At the same time, their comments may be invited on any relevant titles from the suggestion cards already on file.

When the lists are received, they must be checked by the catalogue to avoid unintentional duplication and any titles not already in the suggestion file written out on cards with full details. If these were not given and the librarian cannot readily trace them, help may be sought from the local bookseller patronized by the library. For particulars of foreign books, it is usually better to apply to a firm which specializes in them;

the prices quoted should be turned into English money. Members of staff should be asked to examine books, if possible, before recommending them; some, however, may have to be put on the list before they have been seen. The cards for these books should be marked "Wanted on approval" to remind the librarian to obtain copies immediately before the meeting. If this is done only those not passed will have to be returned.

SUGGESTION AND ORDER FILE

The cards in the suggestion file need to be sorted according to subject, the divisions being shown by guide cards with small tabs; within the subject groups the cards will be put alphabetically by author. As, however, it is not likely that all the titles which have been noted will be presented for consideration at any one meeting, a further division becomes necessary. This is effected by the use of another set of guide cards with wider tabs than those used for subjects; the cards retained for future reference having in front of them a wide-tabbed card marked "Suggestions"; the cards for books to be considered at the next meeting having a similar card marked "For Committee." Additional wide-tabbed guide cards can be added to the file as the suggestion cards are moved along according to the stage which the books represented have reached in the process of acquisition.

The list to be sent to the members of the committee has then only to be prepared from the cards behind the guide marked "For Committee." The librarian will find it convenient to retain a copy of the typed list on which to record the decisions of the meeting. After the meeting the suggestion cards will be re-sorted according to the marked list and the cards for

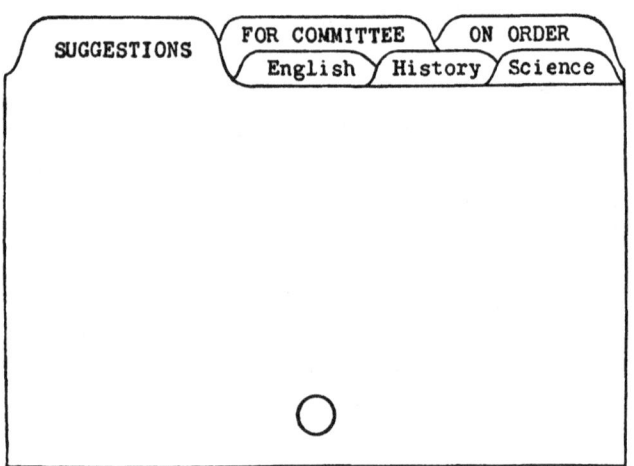
GUIDE CARDS FOR SUGGESTION FILE

books not passed returned to the "Suggestions" division. The cards remaining in the "Committee" division will be arranged according to the placing of the orders. When the orders, which should be in duplicate, have been made out, the cards are moved onwards to a division for books "On order." The file of cards is now well on its way to becoming a complete "Suggestion and order file." It may be useful to summarize here all the headings, both those already mentioned and those to be discussed later, that are likely to be required on the guide cards. They are:—

Suggestions, with sub-guides for subjects.
For Committee.
On order.
Outstanding.
Replacements.
Periodicals.

BOOK BUYING

School libraries which can get their books by requisition will probably obtain the majority by this means, though they are usually at liberty to order secondhand books direct. When the Local Education Authority is recognized as a trading organization, the library will benefit by the special prices on books obtained by requisition. In schools where no such advantage is gained by ordering from one source, there are, very occasionally, regrettable restrictions on the placing of orders which hamper judicious buying. A knowledge of the various markets in which books may be bought will help to secure the best value for the money spent. It is not getting good value to buy a book cheaply if it wears out quickly and soon needs rebinding or replacing. If it is a book of which the interest is likely to be short-lived, the cheap copy may serve, but in buying books which the library must always have, it should be remembered that many binders make a speciality of supplying books in extra strong bindings. The books are ordered direct from the binder, and the small extra initial expense for the "library binding" will be less than the cost of the book as published, plus cost of rebinding. These "library bindings" are specially useful for standard fiction and series of the cheaper kind, such as the *Home University Library*. *Everyman's Library* is issued by the publishers in a library binding obtainable through any bookseller which, for appearance and wear, is worth more than the extra shilling charged. Lighter fiction may, for the most part, be obtained from the binders in "facsimile bindings" which reproduce the publishers' casing and avoid the dullness of uniformity while giving greatly increased durability. Less durable but also useful are the strengthened publishers' cases for which the binders charge a few pence extra for each volume.

The large circulating libraries sell off a considerable portion of their stock when six months old, their agreement with the publishers not permitting them to do so sooner. Hence the importance of noting month as well as year of publication. If the book wanted is about the right age, it is always worth while to inquire if a copy is available even if it has not actually been listed as an ex-library book, but the inquiry must not be left too long as the stocks are quickly sold out. Biographies and books of travel may be obtained to advantage in this way; also fiction if discretion is exercised. A discount is usually allowed to schools.

Booksellers' remainders are often tempting, and

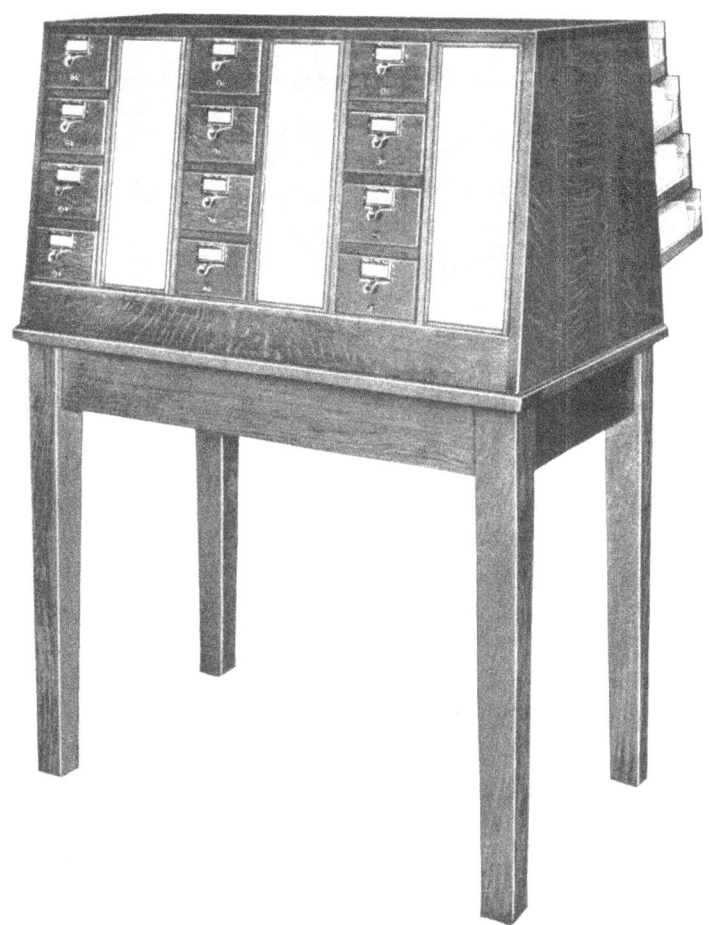

CARD CABINET WITH INCLINED TRAYS
By courtesy of Libraco Ltd.

some bargains may be found, but it is not good policy to order a book unless it will serve a definite purpose.

Out-of-print books and copies of expensive standard works may be sought for among the secondhand booksellers, always with the stipulation that they shall report only clean and perfect copies.

RECEIPT OF BOOKS

As the books are received the librarian checks them by the cards and, having also checked the price, marks the entry on the invoice with a tick, unless there is some discrepancy in edition or price. If so, it is as well to refer to the carbon copy of the order to see that there was no mistake in typing before communicating with the bookseller. If all particulars are correct, the cards may be put temporarily in the front of the file until the books are ready to be added to stock (see Chapter VI). When all the items are passed as correct, the invoice may be initialled and filed. There will usually be one or two books which for some reason cannot be supplied immediately. The cards for these should have the reason for non-delivery entered on them and be filed behind another guide card "Outstanding." This division will also take cards for books for which the order is being held over until they are obtainable at a reduced price. A glance through these cards when looking at lists of secondhand books is often a useful reminder of items wanted.

REPLACEMENTS

Notes of the edition and binding preferred for standard authors may be kept in the file to ensure that uniformity is maintained when odd volumes are ordered as replacements. Books needing replacing may also be noted down for purchase as opportunity offers.

GIFTS

In some schools gifts are a welcome but spasmodic source of addition to the book stock; in others there is a steady flow of books from past and leaving pupils. Where the tradition exists that each pupil on leaving shall give a book, this outlay may be directed towards the systematic building up of the library by displaying lists of "Libri desiderati." Donors should, in any case, be asked to consult the librarian before sending books, and if a miscellaneous collection is offered, the librarian should reserve the right to dispose of any items not required. Gifts, after being suitably acknowledged, will be added to the library and the donor's name inscribed on the book-plate or on a separate donation label.

PERIODICALS

Even if only a few periodicals are taken, some check on their receipt is necessary. Cards 5 by 3 inches are really large enough for the purpose. The same ruling will serve for both monthlies and weeklies, one card lasting six months for weeklies and six years for

CARD FOR MONTHLIES

STUDIO (due end previous month)   2/-

	Jan.	Feb.	Mar.	Apr.	May	June	July	Aug.	Sept.	Oct.	Nov.	Dec.
1935	✓	✓	✓	✓								
1936												
1937												

CARD FOR WEEKLIES

NATURE   Sat. (due Fri.)   1/-

	Jan.	Feb.	Mar.	Apr.	May	June
1935	5 ✓	2 ✓	2 ✓	6	4	1
	12 ✓	9 ✓	9 ✓	13	11	8
	19 ✓	16 ✓	16 ✓	20	18	15
	26 ✓	23 ✓	23 ✓	27	25	22
			30			29

monthlies. A tick in the appropriate square is all that is required to indicate receipt. A rubber stamp can be used to mark the periodicals as library property.

On the back of the card, the following details can be given: name of agent, whether back numbers are bound, filed, or sold, or sent to any particular department of the school. If an annual subscription is paid, the period covered; amount and date of payment should also appear here. If payment is made terminally, it is more convenient to draw a red line on the face of the card after the space for last issue, and mark "Paid." It is then easy to check the number of copies which should be charged. When volumes of periodicals are bound, they should be added to stock like any other book.

CHAPTER VI

ADDITION TO STOCK AND RECORDS OF STOCK

WHEN books have been received and checked, they must be brought into stock and prepared for circulation. It is as well to decide on a definite order of processes so as to avoid passing over any and to work, stage by stage, on a batch of books.

All books received in new condition should be opened at intervals and pressed with the finger down the back fold beginning at either end and working towards the centre; this eases the back and makes it less liable to break. Any serious error in make-up will probably be detected in so doing. Most ordinary editions are issued with the edges of the pages trimmed and free, but when opening a book one should be on the look-out for any pages that the binder's knife has missed and cut these with a paper-knife. If the edges have not been trimmed, it may be necessary first to examine the book to see if it is perfect, then to cut the edges, and then go through the book to make it open easily. If now, or even later, the book should be found to be imperfect, it is quite possible to get the bookseller to return it for the publisher's binder to make the necessary correction.

The classification numbers have to be determined (see Chapter VII) and pencilled in the books. The best

ADDITION TO AND RECORDS OF STOCK

place for the classification number is the back of the title-page; in this position it will be preserved when the book is rebound. Then should follow entry in the accession register and the recording of the accession number in ink or indelible pencil either above or below the classification number.

THE ACCESSION REGISTER

The accession register is the library's basic record in which each book is entered as received, irrespective of subject or source whence obtained. It provides a complete inventory of the stock, shows the annual additions, and is a simple way of accounting for expenditure. As it is the one permanent record, it is best kept in a strongly bound book. The value of the accession register is so great in comparison with the small amount of time required to keep it that school librarians who do not keep such a register are seriously urged to do so.

The lines in the accession register are numbered consecutively, and each volume as it is received is entered on the first vacant line, the number for that line being the accession number of the book. By giving a separate number to each volume as well as to each copy of a work, the accession number becomes its own peculiar mark and alone is sufficient to identify the item.

The rulings given show all the headings required by a school library. The details of vendor and price having been obtained from the order cards, these may

LEFT-HAND PAGE OF ACCESSION REGISTER

Number	Author	Title and Volume
1436	Morris	Practical harmony
1437	Tansley	Elements of plant biology
1438	Bradley	Shakespearean tragedy
1439	Shakespeare	Works (Aldine ed.) vol.1
1440	,,	,, 2

RIGHT-HAND PAGE OF ACCESSION REGISTER

Class	Date of Publication	Condition	Donor or Vendor	Price £ s. d.	Date of Receipt	Remarks
781	1935	cloth	requisition	5 6	30.6.35	
581	1935	cloth	,,	10 —	,,	
820	1929	2nd hd.	Blackwell	9 —	1.7.35	
820	1875	cloth	Chairman of Governors	— —	,,	
820	,,	,,	,,	— —	,,	

be destroyed. Ready-ruled accession registers are sold by Libraco, 62 Cannon Street, London, E.C.2. As each book is entered in the register, the accession number should be written below the classification number on the back of the title-page.

Various experiments have been made in keeping the record of additions without using an accession register but, unless great care is exercised, errors easily arise and such methods are not recommended for school libraries. The librarian of a small library may feel that an accession register is unnecessary, but small libraries become big libraries and the accession register is a convenient record of growth, besides being valuable in other ways. Certainly if duplicate copies of books are acquired, the accession numbers will be found most useful in distinguishing them. Moreover, when one is asked, as sometimes happens, for a book about which the inquirer knows little more than that it was bought some months ago, a glance through the accession register is almost the only hope of tracing the title required.

When a library is being reorganized and no records of purchase have been kept, it is hardly worth while to make individual entries for the existing stock. After weeding out and classifying, the books can be given consecutive numbers and the inclusive numbers for each main class carried into the accession register as so many volumes brought into account.

HEADINGTON SCHOOL FOR GIRLS, OXFORD:
THE LIBRARY IN 1933
By courtesy of the Head Mistress

THE HIGH SCHOOL FOR GIRLS, BRIDLINGTON:
THE LIBRARY IN 1926
*By courtesy of Miss E. Drummond and Miss M. Muir
Photo: Turner and Drinkwater, Hull*

THE SHELF-LIST

After entry in the accession register there follows entry in the shelf-list. The shelf-list is used for checking the library stock; in it the entries are arranged in the order in which the books stand on the shelves. If any are shelved in a special place on account of size, or for any other reason are kept in a parallel classification (see p. 86), they are entered according to their position. In this way a shelf-list differs from a classified catalogue in which all books with the same classification number are entered together, no matter if they are some distance apart on the shelves. The shelf-list can be made to serve as a class-catalogue by double entry of books shelved out of order, writing in red the titles where they would come in exact classified order and in black where they actually stand, the red entries being disregarded when checking the shelves. In this way the shelf-list can be used as a temporary classified catalogue of subjects until such time as an alphabetical subject catalogue (see Chapter VIII) can be made.

The shelf-list can conveniently be kept in a medium-sized loose-leaf book which allows about a dozen entries to a page. The book form is handy for checking and single entries cannot get misplaced. If there are only a few entries to a page, the labour of re-writing when there is no room to insert a title in the correct position is minimized. It can be reduced still further by leaving

SHELF-LIST

ENGLISH LITERATURE, 1500–1599   820H5

Author	Title	Number of Vols.	Accession Number	Remarks
Lyly	Euphues		1072	
Shakespeare	Works (Aldine ed.)	12	1439–50	
	Arden ed. As you like it		501	
	Coriolanus		516	
	Hamlet		502	
	New Hudson. As you like it		659	
	Shakespearean tragedy		1438	
	Shakespeare commentaries, vol 1		1337	
	,, ,, ,, 3		1338	Missing 27.3.34
Bradley				
Gervinus				
Spenser	Poetical works		912	
Webster	Plays (Mermaid)		706	

lines where additions are likely to occur. Some libraries use their order cards for the shelf-list, but the card form is not so convenient, and the details of publisher and price only distract the eye from seizing on the essential items.

It will be observed that, for the shelf-list, a complete set with consecutive accession numbers is concentrated into one line, whereas an incomplete work has a line to a volume. Works in progress should also have a line a volume. In the column for the title, it is useful to give a brief note of series or edition as this helps one to find the volume quickly when checking. The arrangement of the entries in the example shows how the suggestion made on p. 81 for a simple chronological classification of literary texts would work out.

THE CATALOGUE

The books must next be catalogued (see Chapter VIII). The catalogue cards need not be filed immediately they are written, but they should be in their places before the books are put on the shelves.

PREPARATION OF BOOKS FOR ISSUE

After cataloguing, only the finishing processes remain to be done, such as writing the issue card if used and pasting in the pocket to take it (see p. 106), putting the classification number on the back of the book (see p. 87), and pasting the library book-plate on the inside of the front cover. If a space is provided on the book-plate in which the accession number is given this will be a help to borrowers; libraries which do not mark their books on the back frequently put the classification number here as well. Both numbers will already have been recorded on the back of the title-page, and are easily written on the book-plate before pasting it on the cover. It is useful if the final process is one which leaves its mark on the book, such as numbering on the back or book-plating; this serves then as a clear indication of completion.

Attention may be drawn to the new books by putting a list on the library notice-board and displaying the books on a special shelf for a week or so. It is a good plan to notify members of staff or others who have a prior claim on certain of the books when the additions are about to be released for issue so that they may secure any book of special interest to them. Two or three days after making the announcement that the new books may be taken out, any that are left should be put in their places on the shelves.

WITHDRAWALS AND REPLACEMENTS

As books wear out or are superseded they will have to be withdrawn or replaced. If an accurate account is to be kept of the library stock, a record of books withdrawn must be made. The withdrawal register is the complement of the accession register. When a book is withdrawn, a red ink cross is put against the number in the accession register and in the column for remarks the word "Withdrawn" and the date. Entries in the withdrawal register can be quite brief, but should include a running withdrawal number for each volume, the author, title, accession number, the reason for withdrawal, and date of withdrawal. All cards for books withdrawn must be removed from the catalogues and the shelf-list entry cancelled. A rubber stamp "Withdrawn" is useful for cancelling the bookplate to prevent any possible misunderstanding on the part of persons who may come across the book afterwards. As a general rule, it is better not to use up withdrawn numbers for new books.

When a new edition or clean copy of a book is substituted for the existing copy, it is usually sufficient to write "Replaced" and the date in the remarks column of the accession register. If, however, a statement of the amount spent on replacements is required, it may be advisable to keep a replacement register. The new copy is given the same accession number as the displaced one, and if there are important revisions these must be noted on the catalogue cards and shelf-list.

STOCKTAKING

From time to time it will be necessary to take stock of the library. For this the shelf-list is used. The checking of the shelves can most easily be done by two people working together, one reading from the list and the other finding the books. The titles of books not found can be jotted down on a spare page of the shelf-list, or if the shelf-list is on cards one of the small metal indicator clips sold for commercial use may be slipped on the card. A good many of the books wanted will be found in other sections when these come to be checked, and one has to remember to take into account any books put aside for mending or sending to the binder. If, as is perfectly possible, the checking is done without calling in the books, the issue register will have to be examined in conjunction with the books on the shelves. If inexperienced help is used for checking, a careful scrutiny of the shelves for titles on the list of missing books should be made, as it is remarkable how many of these will have been overlooked, and will be found in or near their correct places. After a thorough hunt and making inquiries of persons who might have had the books, the word "missing" and the date will be entered in the remarks column of the shelf-list against any titles outstanding. Books often reappear after an interval, so, unless the need is urgent, it is as well to postpone replacement for some time. If after two or three years the books are still missing, and there has been no demand for them, it may be advisable to withdraw the entries for them from the library records.

Shelf-checking affords a good opportunity for overhauling the stock, and one should be on the watch for volumes which do not seem to justify the space they occupy, with a view to bringing up later the question of their withdrawal. It is possible, also, that shelf-checking will direct attention to subjects which are not represented, and to works which ought to be considered for addition.

STATISTICS OF STOCK

The accession and withdrawal registers will, between them, yield any necessary statistics of stock, the existing stock at any given time being found by subtracting the last running number in the withdrawal register from the last number in the accession register. If the end of the statistical year is marked in both registers, it is only necessary to subtract the last number for the previous year from the last number of the current year to obtain the year's additions and withdrawals. Without the registers it will not be so easy to arrive at the figures.

SUMMARY OF PROCESSES OF ADDITION

A list of the processes described in Chapters V–VIII is here given for convenience in ready reference.

> Title suggested.
> Checked by catalogue.
> Suggestion card written.
> Cards arranged in order.
> List typed.
> Selection made by Committee or the Head.
> Cards sorted according to decision.
> Orders made out.
> Books received and checked for edition and price.
> Order cards put in front of file, or in the books.
> Books examined, opened and cut.

Classified.
Entered in Accession register.
Entered in Shelf-list.
Catalogued.
Book-plated.
Issue card written, pocket and, if required, date label affixed.
Displayed.
Catalogue cards filed.
Proposers notified that books are available.
Books put in permanent places.

CHAPTER VII

CLASSIFICATION

THE great increase in the usefulness of a library that results from a suitable systematic arrangement on the shelves makes it most important to consider carefully the form of classification to be adopted. The main object of any scheme of classification is to bring close together the books treating of the same subject. No system can collect in one place all the books that any one student will need, but if the greater number of them form a distinct block then the classification is serving its purpose.

In order to mark out the blocks or classes, some form of numbering or other notation is required, all books on the same subject bearing the same classification number. When many books on a subject are added and more room for it is required, the books in the succeeding classes can be moved along into a new case if necessary, but no alteration in numbering is involved because the subjects will still be in the same relative position. The old method of allotting so many shelves or cases to a class and numbering by cases and shelves necessitates much changing of the numbers when books have to be moved. In colleges and schools where there are collections of old and valuable books, these have generally been numbered by shelves and might well remain so, as this part of the library will not grow much. The reclassification of the modern books on a flexible system should, however, certainly be undertaken as it will more than repay in increased usefulness the labour of the change-over. Having the two different systems will not be found to be so serious a difficulty as might be feared.

When books are numbered by subjects, some accepted order will be necessary for arranging the books which bear the same number; this is provided by following the alphabetical sequence of authors' surnames.

CHOICE OF SCHEME

The choice of a classification scheme for a school library lies between one which is in common use in libraries of a general nature and an arrangement which more closely reflects the trend of school studies and interests. In so far as school is a preparation for later life, there is much to be said in favour of adopting a scheme such as the *Decimal Classification*[1] of Melvil Dewey which is the system followed by the majority of Public Libraries. Pupils who have made intelligent use of a school library arranged on this method should be able to find their way round the shelves of most Public Libraries. It is undoubtedly to the advantage of readers and library officials that there should be one standardized system. It cannot, however, be denied that the Decimal Classification cuts across the lines of

[1] See Selected References.

the school curriculum. Those who adopt it must be prepared to accept, for some subjects, a form of arrangement which is not entirely convenient in order to obtain the advantages of conformity in method with libraries which serve a wider public.

The most frequently criticized of Dewey's divisions from the school point of view are those for languages, classical studies, and geography; moreover, some school librarians would prefer a strictly chronological arrangement of literature. If it is felt that the divisions which run counter to school requirements make it impossible to adopt the scheme as it stands, it will be better not to alter the meanings of the numbers for subjects but to follow some other arrangement which embodies the desired features. Many of the features likely to be required will be found in the scheme designed by Miss E. S. Fegan for the Cheltenham Ladies' College and published in her *School Libraries*.[1] The original edition is now nearly exhausted, but it is hoped that it may be possible to bring out a separate issue of the classification schedules somewhat extended and fully indexed.

A very interesting adaptation of the Library of Congress scheme of classification has been worked out for his own library by Mr. F. C. Perry, of the Bristol Grammar School. This, he says, has stood the test of six years of practical application to a fairly large and growing library.

[1] See Selected References.

Some school librarians may consider drawing up their own scheme of classification, and a few have worked out schemes which appear to be satisfactory. It may, however, be worth pointing out that while it is comparatively easy to draft an outline which will serve for a moderate number of books, it is by no means easy to ensure that it will answer equally well when the library has grown.

Whatever system of classification is chosen, it should be one that provides a greater number of divisions than are actually needed at the date of adoption. If the classification is begun on lines that are too broad and simple, heterogeneous collections of books will accumulate at many of the numbers. Further subdivision will then have to be undertaken, involving the addition of symbols for the subdivisions both in the books and on the catalogue cards. Dewey has pertinently remarked, "Whether there are one or a thousand books on any topic, they take no more room on the shelves if classified minutely and the work is done once for all."

THE DECIMAL CLASSIFICATION

The Decimal Classification[1] of Melvil Dewey is published in three degrees of fullness: the complete classification, the abridged classification, and the primer. Schools which wish to adopt the scheme are advised not to begin with anything less detailed than

[1] See Selected References.

the abridged form, and this they should buy. None but the largest school libraries are likely to require to possess the complete form of the classification. For general guidance in applying the scheme, the reader is referred to the paragraphs on assigning class numbers in the explanatory introduction to *The Abridged Decimal Classification*[1] and to such classified catalogues as *Books for Youth*[2] and *1,000 Books for the Senior High School Library*.[3]

The Abridged Decimal Classification[4] has a very detailed alphabetical index of subjects which occupies twice as many pages as the classification tables, and is a great asset. Important as the index is, it is not intended as a substitute for the tables. Indeed, classifiers are strongly urged to make it a rule not to assign any number to a book without reference to the tables. These alone can be relied on to reveal the context of a number. There is, for example, a place for the subject "Colour" in the Science and in the Fine Arts classes of the Decimal scheme; both these numbers and several others as well are shown in the index. It is most necessary when selecting a number to take into account the nature of the class within which it falls.

The index is to be used as a means of ensuring that possible placings have not been overlooked and as a check on the consistent assignment of numbers. It is the great value of the index for these purposes that

[1] See Selected References. [2] Ibid. [3] Ibid. [4] Ibid.

makes it inadvisable to alter the meanings of the numbers because the index entries are thereby invalidated.

An abbreviated form of the index, together with the first hundred divisions of the classification, is issued by Libraco Ltd. under the title *How to find a book*.[1] It has been found useful to supply copies of this for the guidance of readers.

OUTLINE OF THE DECIMAL CLASSIFICATION

The terms or headings of the Decimal scheme are called classes, divisions, sections, and subsections. The classes are numbered in hundreds, the divisions in tens, the sections in units, and the subsections are marked by figures after a decimal point. School libraries will not, normally, have books which fall in certain of the divisions. These, therefore, have been omitted from the following synopsis. *The Abridged Decimal Classification* should be followed for the numbers for sections and subsections. In some instances it may be desirable to adopt a few additional subsections from the complete scheme, in others it may be found that the headings given under some divisions in the abridged scheme are not likely to be required.

Any headings adopted which are additional to those printed in the abridged scheme should be written in where they belong in the library's copy of the scheme;

[1] See Selected References.

they should also be noted in the index. When it is decided that certain subsections shall not be used, these should be pencilled through in the tables. If every number is invariably looked up in the tables it will hardly be necessary to make alterations in the index.

THE DECIMAL SCHEME IN OUTLINE

000	GENERAL WORKS.	
010	Bibliography.	
020	Library economy.	
030	General encyclopaedias.	
040	General collected essays.	
050	General periodicals.	
100	PHILOSOPHY.	
140	Philosophical systems.	
150	Psychology.	
160	Logic.	
170	Ethics.	
200	RELIGION.	
220	Bible.	
230	Christian doctrine.	
240	Devotional and personal religion.	
260	The Church, its institutions and work.	
270	Religious history.	
290	Non-Christian religions, mythology.	
300	SOCIOLOGY.	
310	Statistics.	
320	Political science.	
330	Economics.	

CLASSIFICATION

SOCIOLOGY—*continued*.

340	Law.
350	Administration.
360	Associations and institutions.
370	Education.
380	Commerce, communication.
390	Customs, popular life.

(Books on the historical aspect of social life are most usefully classified at the history number.)

400	LANGUAGES.
420	English.
430	German.
440	French.
450	Italian.
460	Spanish.
470	Latin.
480	Greek.
490	Other languages.

500	SCIENCE.
510	Mathematics.
520	Astronomy
530	Physics.
540	Chemistry.
550	Geology.
560	Palaeontology.
570	Biology.
580	Botany.
590	Zoology.

600	USEFUL ARTS.
610	Medicine.
620	Engineering.
630	Agriculture.
640	Domestic economy.

USEFUL ARTS—*continued*.

650 Business methods.
660 Chemical technology.
670 Manufactures.
680 Mechanical crafts
690 Building.

700 FINE ARTS.
710 Gardening.
720 Architecture.
730 Sculpture.
740 Drawing and design.
750 Painting.
760 Engraving.
770 Photography.
780 Music.
790 Games and amusements.

800 LITERATURE.
810 American.
820 English.
830 German.
840 French.
850 Italian.
860 Spanish.
870 Latin.
880 Greek.
890 Other literatures.

900 HISTORY.
910 Geography.
920 Biography.
  (If it is preferred to distribute biographies under the subjects they illustrate then 920 will be used only for lives which do not bear specially on any subject.)

HISTORY—*continued*.

930		Ancient history.
940	⎡	Europe.
950	⎢	Asia.
960	⎨ Modern	Africa.
970	⎢	North America.
980	⎢	South America.
990	⎣	Oceania and polar regions.

In the literature class, works on the history and criticism of a literature precede the works of the writers of that literature and, in small libraries, receive the division number only, e.g. 820 English literature. An additional figure for literary form, such as Poetry or Drama, is used for texts. It would, however, be possible to arrange these by period by omitting the numbers for literary form and using instead the letter "H" (for hundred) followed by the figure for the hundreds. The period 1500-1599 would thus be represented by H5, this symbol would be added to the Dewey number for the literature. By this means the works of Shakespeare and Spenser would stand side by side at 820H5 instead of being separated. This proposal complies with the condition laid down in the introduction to the Decimal scheme that any symbols for changed meanings which appear in print must be such that they cannot be mistaken for Dewey numbers.

The chronological arrangement, besides following the natural method of study, avoids the difficulty of classifying the works of authors like Goldsmith who have written in almost every form. By dividing by hundreds rather than by centuries the way is left open for carrying out the division to periods of fifty or even ten years, this merely requiring the addition of the figure for the decade. This further division would probably be needed only for the seventeen and eighteen hundreds, thus H8 would stand for 1800–1849 and H85 for 1850–1899. Criticisms of an author should be given the same number as his works, and should follow them on the shelves. The examples given have been taken from English literature, but foreign literatures would be treated in the same way.

Books in a foreign language on a definite subject are usually given the number for that subject, and translations of a foreign literary text have the number that the original would be given. Common sense will, nevertheless, indicate some variations according to the purpose for which a book is required and the linguistic attainments of readers. It may be advisable, sometimes, to place an original text which has definite subject-matter with the literature of the language in which it is written, and to put a translation at the number for the subject. Machiavelli's *The Prince* is an instance in point. If the library possesses the book only in the original, the subject classification will probably have the prior claim. Translations of literary works from a language not studied as a school subject may be classified with English literature.

In the history class, Dewey gives the British Empire

the same number (942) as England. This is not convenient for English libraries and various suggestions have been made, from time to time, for distinguishing books on the Empire. The simplest way to overcome the difficulty would be to add the letters "BE" (for British Empire) to the number for England.

OUTLINE OF THE CHELTENHAM SCHEME

The Cheltenham scheme follows the grouping of subjects as they are usually taught in schools. Each language is followed by its literature; literature is arranged in a simple chronological sequence so that the poetry, drama, and prose of any one period stand together; there is a section for classical studies which assembles all works on classical subjects with the exception of ancient history which cannot well be separated from the History class; the various aspects of geography—political, physical, and commercial—stand in close proximity to each other.

The main classes are marked by letters and the divisions by Arabic numerals. For convenience in summarizing, the latter are here grouped under Roman numerals which do not form part of the symbols to be assigned to books. For instance, in the full scheme, the group S.1 is divided into:

1. General works on art.
2. Theory and philosophy of art.
3. Periodicals.

The marks to be applied to books are S1, S2, S3.

THE CHELTENHAM SCHEME IN OUTLINE

A THEOLOGY.
 I   Bible, Biblical study.
 II Religious history.
 III Christian theology.
 IV Comparative and non-Christian religions.

B MORAL SCIENCE.
 I   History of philosophy.
 II Mental philosophy.
 III Moral philosophy.

C SOCIOLOGY.
 I   Government and law.
 II Economics.
 III Education.
 IV Domestic economy.
 V   Customs, folklore.

D HISTORY.
 I   General works.
 II Universal history.
 III Ancient history.
 IV Modern history.

E ENGLISH.
 I   Language and history of literature.
 II Old English.
 III English authors.
 IV Colonial and American authors.

F FRENCH.

G GERMAN.

H ITALIAN.

J SPANISH.

K CLASSICS.
  I   Language and history of literature.
  II Greek authors.
  III Latin authors.
  IV Archaeology and antiquities.

R SCIENCE AND MATHEMATICS.
  I   General scientific treatises.
  II   Astronomy.
  III Mathematics.
  IV   Physics.
  V   Chemistry.
  VI   Geography and geology.
  VII Biology.
  VIII Botany.
  IX   Zoology.
  X   Applied science, technology.

S FINE ARTS.
  I   General treatises.
  II   Architecture.
  III Sculpture.
  IV   Drawing, painting and allied arts.
  V   Music.
  VI   Minor arts.

Z GENERALIA.
  I   General encyclopaedias.
  II   General periodicals.
  III General collections.
  IV   Bibliography.
  V   Library economy.

THE PROCESS OF CLASSIFYING

When reorganizing an unclassified library, it is best to begin the work of applying the numbers by sorting the books roughly into main classes. It can then be seen how they can be spaced out in the bookcases so that the numbers run consecutively with as little dodging about as possible. Many school librarians like to keep together in one portion of the library all such books as encyclopaedias, dictionaries, atlases, and yearbooks, which may be used only in the library. This makes for convenience in reference, and acts as a safeguard against the books being taken out by mistake. If this practice is adopted, the books confined to the library could have a capital R over the classification number; the mark for a Latin dictionary would then be $\frac{R}{473}$ (Dewey) $\frac{R}{K3}$ (Cheltenham). There are sure to be some books which, on account of their height, cannot stand in their proper place. Special shelves are usually assigned for oversize books which are arranged by classification number in a sequence parallel to the main sequence. Sometimes for subjects such as Art on which there are many large books, the bottom shelves of the case can be used for oversize volumes. If desired, a capital F (for folio) over the number can be used to indicate the oversize sequence. In sorting the books, some may be found which are not likely to be used much but which it is thought advisable to keep stored away. A capital S for Store may then be put over the classification number.

The classification numbers should be pencilled in the books, the best place is the back of the title-page. The number is also often written on the book-plate. If many people will replace the books the numbers will be needed on the back of the cover; they should be put at a uniform height from the bottom. Labels are not satisfactory, as they are unsightly and liable to fall off; if used they should be damped on the front side before being pasted on the book. The alternatives are direct writing of the numbers in Reeve's white waterproof ink, or better still by the use of an electric stylus over gold or coloured foil (see p. 117). Numbers on the backs spoil the look of the books but they cannot always be avoided.

When the books have been classified and stand in order on the shelves, adequate guides or labels for the shelves should be prepared, giving the classification numbers and the subjects they represent. Large framed guides in bold letters are generally used over the cases for the main classes, and small slips of the thickness of the shelf for the subdivisions. Labels printed with the Dewey numbers can be obtained from the library suppliers. The shelf labels must be movable and the front edges of the shelves should be grooved to take them. Failing this, the labels may be slipped into metal sides which clip on to the shelf; these are excellent but expensive.

CHAPTER VIII

CATALOGUING

CATALOGUING for school libraries need not be elaborate, though it is important that it should be accurate, and that all essential items should be given. Hasty or incomplete cataloguing has been the bane of many libraries; through it useful information may be lost to view, and even when errors are detected, their correction entails much labour.

The most useful form of catalogue has its entries on standard-sized cards, 5 by 3 inches, either hand-written or typewritten. Hand-written cards, if uniform, clear and neat, look quite well, but typewriting is preferable if there are likely to be successive cataloguers whose writing is strongly individualistic. If the cards are to be typed, the entries should first be made on slips and the cards typed from these. Direct cataloguing on the typewriter, except possibly for fiction, requires a high degree of skill. A black typewriter ribbon, not a purple, should be used.

KINDS OF CATALOGUE

An alphabetical arrangement of authors and subjects, whether in two sequences or combined (see p. 103) is probably the most useful kind of catalogue for schools. In a classified catalogue the entries are arranged in a logical order according to the numerical or other symbols of a classification scheme chosen for the purpose. Alphabetical catalogues only will be discussed here; anyone who wishes to know more about the construction of classified catalogues is referred to Part II of the *Manual of Cataloguing and Indexing*,[1] by J. H. Quinn and H. W. Acomb.

FORM OF ENTRY

The first and most important entry to be made for an alphabetical catalogue is the author entry, so-called because the author's surname stands at the top left-hand corner of the card and is the word which determines the place of the card amongst the other cards in the catalogue. Particulars for the entry should be taken from the title-page, not from the cover, though if there is a different title on the cover, this may be given in parentheses.

The items, taken in order, are:

On the top line

1. Author's surname.
2. Forenames or initials, after a comma. When possible one forename should be given in full. Personal titles, where necessary, are given on this line, but only those of high rank need be entered. Whenever in doubt as to the form of heading previously used, it will be very necessary to

[1] See Selected References.

examine the existing entries. If one person has been entered as Brown, Henry, it will not do to write another entry for him as Brown, H. A., thus making two authors out of one. The reverse of the process has also to be avoided.

3. Classification number at the top right-hand corner. Many libraries put the classification number to the left of the surname, but when the surname is the arranging factor, it is more logical for it to come first.

On the second line, indented

4. Title of book. The title may be abbreviated if this can be done without loss of information. If the title over-runs the line, begin the next line at extreme left.
5. Edition. This is part of the title, and should follow on after it.
6. Series. The name of the series should be given in parentheses. It will usually be found on the half-title preceding the title-page. The series should not be given for sets whose only characteristic in common is their binding, such as World's Classics or Everyman's Library.

Leave a line blank. On next line indented

7. Collation, i.e. statement of physical make-up. The number of volumes if more than one should be given, the number of pages is not necessary. If

CATALOGUING

the book is illustrated, let the term "illus." cover all kinds of illustrations except maps which should be separately specified.

8. Imprint. Publisher and date of publication should be given. School libraries are not likely to have books issued by little-known publishers so that the place of publication is not absolutely necessary. The date of publication is important and, except for music and modern fiction, should always be given. If it does not appear in the book, an approximate date should be assigned and enclosed in square brackets. Sometimes several dates of publication appear on the back of the title-page, the latest of these should be given. Inclusive dates only need be given when volumes of a work have different dates.

On next line

9. Contents. This should be given chiefly for books containing several works or distinct contributions, or when there is definite division of the subject-matter between two or more volumes.

On next line, centred

10. Number of copies of the same edition if more than one, entered in pencil. Different editions should have separate cards. If the accession numbers are required for purposes of identification, they can be obtained from the shelf-list.

The specimen card shown below is for an entirely imaginary work, and has been compounded to show all the details likely to be required. Only rarely will all of these apply to any one entry, but the relevant details should always be given in the same order.

In writing entries, restraint in the use of capitals and stops is advised as this makes the entries easier to read. A full stop should be used after abbreviations,

AUTHOR ENTRY

BROWNRIGG, CYRIL W.　　　　　　942.07

Home life, entertainments and journeyings in Georgian England. 2nd ed. revised. (Social and economic studies.)

2 vols. illus. map. Allen & Unwin, 1933-34. vol. 1 George I & II. vol. 2 George III.

2 copies

O

---

but not after forms like 2nd or 3rd which are contractions. The use of another stop after an abbreviation should be avoided, and also after a bracket, unless required to close the sentence or statement. Any words or figures which are not on the title-page but are added to the title by the cataloguer should be enclosed in square brackets.

When a work which is still in course of publication

is being catalogued, it is sufficient to write "in progress" in pencil where the number of volumes would normally be given and to put a dash after the date of the first volume. The shelf-list (see p. 64) will show which volumes have been received. When the work is completed, the pencil note should be rubbed out and the number of volumes substituted; the date of publication of the last volume must be added after the dash that was left. If desired, the individual titles of volumes may be entered, as they are received, in the "Contents" portion of the catalogue card.

CHOICE OF HEADINGS

Rules governing the headings to be used for the various classes of authors whose names offer difficulties are given in the various cataloguing codes, though as these are not always easy to interpret all school librarians who can are advised to take a course in cataloguing or to seek the help of an expert. When a book may be looked for under some other heading than that chosen, a reference should be made. If the Anglo-American code[1] is followed, it would be useful to note on the blank pages, opposite the rules permitting alternatives, which of them has been adopted, and also to make notes of any exceptions and of illustrative examples showing the form of heading. A detailed discussion of the rules will be found in *Cataloguing*,[2] by H. A. Sharp.

[1] See Selected References. [2] Ibid.

A summary of the rules that most frequently apply is subjoined.

1. Enter a book under the name of the author whether individual or corporate. The author is defined as the person or body responsible for the existence of a book; consequently collected contributions by a number of writers are to be entered under the editor, though if the work is universally known by its title, it may be entered under that, e.g. Cambridge modern history, Oxford Book of English Prose. Anonymous books, of which the author cannot be traced, have to be entered under the first word of the title other than an article.
2. Enter a book written jointly by two authors under the name of the first followed by that of the second. Refer from the second name, e.g. Scott, R., *see* Liddell, Henry G., and Scott, R. If more than two authors, use the form Brown, Robert, *and others*.
3. Enter English compound surnames under the last part of the name, and refer from the first part. This practice is in accordance with the British Museum rules[1] and Cutter's rules[1] and is on the whole preferable to entry under the first part as directed by the Anglo-American code. Many English double-barrelled names

[1] See Selected References.

are not really compounds, the first part being merely a joined-on forename. Foreign compound names should be entered under the first part as that is the customary usage in Continental countries. Refer from any part of a foreign name that might be looked for.

4. Surnames with prefixes must be distinguished from compound names, specially from those which contain a prefix, e.g. Viollet-Le-Duc, Eugène. Enter all English names beginning with a prefix under the prefix, e.g. De la Mare, Walter; De Morgan, William. Enter French names under the prefix when it consists of or contains an article, eg. La Fontaine, Jean de; Des Granges, C. M.; otherwise enter under the part following the prefix, e.g. Musset, Alfred de. Enter Italian and Spanish names under the prefix when it consists of the article alone; also enter under the prefix when it is written with the name as one word whatever the nationality. Enter all other names (principally German and Dutch) under the part following the prefix, e.g. Schiller, Friedrich von.

5. Enter under their forenames saints and other persons known by their forenames only. Enter monarchs, ruling princes, and popes under the name officially assumed.

6. Enter British noblemen under their family names and refer from their titles. Even if it does bring

GRESHAM'S SCHOOL, HOLT: THE LIBRARY IN 1933
Copyright: Raphael Tuck and Sons, Ltd.

some persons under unfamiliar headings, this is the English rule, and should be followed, e.g. Northcote, Stafford H., 1*st earl of Iddesleigh*.

> Iddesleigh, 1st earl of, *see* Northcote, Stafford H.

The American practice of entry under the title presents as many difficulties and has the added disadvantage that when a new title is assumed the catalogue entries have to be changed. There are, however, distinct advantages in entering foreign noblemen under their titles.

7. Enter ecclesiastical dignitaries under their surnames.
8. Enter pseudonymous works under the author's real name when known, and refer from the pseudonym. A few exceptions may be made for writers who habitually use a pseudonym and are universally known by it, e.g. Eliot, George. A record should be kept of such exceptions. In a separate catalogue of fiction, entry under pseudonyms may be much more frequently made.
9. Enter a married woman under the earliest name, not necessarily her maiden name, which she has used as an author, and refer from later names, e.g. Cartwright, Julia (*Mrs.* Henry Ady)

> Ady, Julia (*Mrs.* Henry Ady), *see* Cartwright, Julia.

If a woman does not use her husband's forenames

or initials on the title-page, they need not be given, e.g. Meynell, *Mrs.* Alice.
10. Enter classical writers under the forms adopted in a standard classical dictionary. The British Museum enters ancient Greek writers under the English form of the name.
11. Enter documents published by the authority of governments, whether central or local, or by any of their departments, under the name of the country or area concerned. English libraries frequently enter home government departments directly under the department instead of under Great Britain.
12. Enter the official publications of a society, such as reports and transactions, under the first word other than an article of its corporate name and refer from any other name by which it is known.
13. Enter the publications of an institution, i.e. a body to whom the possession of a building is essential to its organization, such as a university, school, museum, or art gallery, under the name of the place in which the institution is situated. Institutions whose names are distinctive may, however, be entered under their own names, e.g. National Gallery.
14. Enter sacred books and anonymous classics under the English name by which they are known.
15. Enter periodicals under the first word of the title other than an article.

16. Enter year-books and directories under their titles.
17. Enter encyclopaedias and dictionaries under the name of the editor unless decidedly better known by their titles. When entering under the editor a work whose title includes the name of the publisher, refer from the publisher. When entering under the title, refer from the editor.
18. Enter a musical work under the composer, indicating the kind of work, the instruments for which it is set, the key, the opus number, and, if not self-evident, the nature of the score. The titles of musical works may be translated into English.
19. When a book has already been entered under its author, an additional entry under the title may occasionally be given if the book is more likely to be remembered by this. Readers may be expected to know the authors of classic works and books about a subject are better entered under a subject heading, so that added title entries are not needed in these instances.
20. For a book belonging to a distinct series, such as the Loeb Library, an additional entry under the name of the series is useful.

SUBJECT ENTRY

To complete the cataloguing of all books, except works of the imagination, entries under the subjects covered will be required. In alphabetical subject cataloguing a heading chosen by the cataloguer to represent the subject-matter of the book stands at the head of the entry. The place of the card in the catalogue is determined by the first word of the heading. As the subject heading occupies a line it is usual to condense

SUBJECT ENTRY

ENGLAND, SOCIAL LIFE: 18th century. 942.07

Brownrigg, C. W. Home life, entertainments and journeyings in Georgian England. 2nd ed. revised. (Social and economic studies.)

2 vols. illus. map. 1933–34.
vol. 1. George I & II. vol. 2. George III.

2 copies.

---

the entry. Instead of forenames, the author's initials only are given, the title of the book is run straight on after the author, and the publisher is omitted.

The specimen card shows a convenient way of setting out the entry. It will be noticed that the subject heading "England, Social life" is given in capitals followed by a colon and the sub-heading "18th century." The heading should be so contrived that only one sub-heading is necessary. The author's name is made to stand out by indenting the second and third lines of the title by the space of three letters.

A subject heading should be chosen with care, as it must fit the content of the book under consideration as closely as possible and yet be in accord with the general trend of the literature of the subject so that it will also fit other books. For this reason it is advisable to follow the headings adopted in some list of proved value such as the *Subject index*[1] of the London Library or the *List of subject headings for small libraries*,[2] edited by M. E. Sears. The London Library *Subject index* is unfortunately only obtainable by members, and is expensive, but it is particularly valuable not only for the well-chosen headings but also for the entries of books which are of great assistance in determining the appropriate headings for like titles.

As an instance of the two main principles to be observed in the choice of subject headings the example used for the specimen card will serve. The heading does fit the content of the book as closely as possible. If the heading were "Social life" it would be too general as this should only be used for books on social life not limited to any one country. It is not always easy to pin a book down to its exact subject, and the natural tendency is to enter it under a wider and more inclusive heading. Subject cataloguers will find it necessary to guard strenuously against this tendency. The heading given in the example will

[1] See Selected References.   [2] Ibid.

accommodate other books. If the exact dates covered, 1714-1820, were given in the heading, it would probably be suitable only for this one book.

Combined headings can sometimes be used, e.g. "Money and currency," but many books can be properly covered only by making more than one entry. A book on drawing and engraving must be entered both under "Drawing" and under "Engraving." A combined heading would not fit the general trend of books, as it is more usual to find the subjects treated separately. Personal names used as subject headings are governed by the same rules as author headings.

To complete the subject cataloguing, references connecting the various headings are desirable. These may be "see" or "see also" references. A "see" reference is made from a heading which is not to be used to one that is to be used, e.g.

POLITICAL ECONOMY, *see* ECONOMICS.

A "see also" reference is made from a wide heading to one less inclusive, and also between allied headings which are yet sufficiently different not to be treated as synonyms, e.g.

ART, *see also* DRAWING.
PAINTING, *see also* DRAWING.

These references should be made when a book on the subject referred to is being catalogued, otherwise one is in danger of sending the reader to headings under which there are as yet no entries.

Analytical subject entries, that is entries for portions only of books, are undoubtedly very valuable for small libraries, especially if made for collected essays and bound journals, as they reveal information on subjects

ANALYTICAL SUBJECT ENTRY

BOTANY, NORWAY.	914.8
Tindall, E. Wild Flowers of Norway. (*In* Keary, C. F. Norway and the Norwegians, p. 374-494.) 1892.	

on which there may not be books available. They add, however, very considerably to the labour of compiling the catalogue.

When the portion analysed is by the author of the whole work, the formula "*In his*" may be used to avoid repeating the name.

When the cataloguing of a book has been completed it is useful to note on the back of the principal entry card, usually the author card, the headings under which additional entries have been made. This "tracing" is extremely helpful if the classification number is changed or the entries for the book have to be withdrawn, as all cards relating to it can quickly be found. References should not be "traced."

ARRANGEMENT

The entries when made can be arranged in two alphabetical sequences, one of authors and titles, the other of subjects, or they can be combined in one alphabet forming a dictionary catalogue. In school libraries it will generally be found that it is more practical to make one catalogue of authors and another of subjects.

Before filing the cards, it is as well to make sure that one has mastered the conventions for alphabetizing recognized by cataloguers and indexers, such as that for names beginning with Mac, Mc, or M', which are all arranged as if spelled Mac in full. The directions for arranging cards given by Susan Akers[1] are good and clear, and rather simpler than those of Cutter.[2]

STAGES IN COMPILATION

If it is impossible to catalogue a library fully at first, the shelf-list can be so constructed that it will serve temporarily as a substitute (see p. 64). In smaller libraries this may be all that is required for some time. If possible, however, an author catalogue

[1] See Selected References.   [2] Ibid.

should be provided at the start, or at any rate at the earliest possible moment. Subject cataloguing can, if necessary, be postponed. When the library is fully catalogued, the shelf-list will revert to its proper function as a check-list for official use.

CATALOGUING EQUIPMENT

As the catalogue is a permanent record, it is worth while to use materials of good quality. The cards should be tough and strong with a hard surface, and they should be perfectly true. Only those cut on a rotary machine will be found to be free from the slight inequalities which make cards difficult to consult. Some guide cards with projecting tabs will be needed. They can be obtained with tabs of various widths, and also with the divisions of the alphabet ready printed and protected by celluloid. Both entry cards and guide cards should be of standard size, which it is worth noting is based on measurement in centimetres, and is actually rather less than 5 by 3 inches. Cards of the full measure in inches will not go into a standard-sized cabinet drawer. Card cabinets have been discussed in Chapter II under the heading "Miscellaneous Equipment." For those who prefer a book form, sheaf catalogues provide the necessary adjustability. As the slips on which the entries are made are quite thin, they can be typed in duplicate. The card form, however, seems to be more generally preferred.

CHAPTER IX

ISSUE AND RECALL OF BOOKS

It will hardly be necessary, under ordinary circumstances, to record the use made of books read in the library itself; a little observation will determine whether this is about average or on the increase. Every book or other item taken out of the library, even if only for a few minutes, must be entered. An exercise book, ruled in columns, is all that is necessary for the entry of periodicals and newspapers borrowed; borrowers generally cancel their own entries. Returned books should be left on the librarian's desk, or a table or shelf set apart for the purpose, so that the librarian or his assistants can cancel the entries. There are various ways of registering book issues which show automatically who has a book, when a book is due back, or what books a given person has. In choosing between them, it is important to bear in mind the factor it is most desired to emphasize.

ISSUE REGISTER

Method 1.—For small libraries a good-sized exercise book would suffice. It would be divided into sections according to the letters of the alphabet, and the pages ruled in columns for author, title, accession number, borrower, date taken out, date returned. Books are entered in the sections according to initial letter of author's surname. This shows sufficiently clearly both who has a given book and what books have not been returned to time. If a loose-leaf book is used, sheets can be removed when all entries on them have been cancelled.

Method 2.—This is a "card in book" system similar to that in general use in public libraries, but it does not require a borrower's ticket. The functions of a borrower's ticket are to identify the borrower and to limit the issue of books to one or two at a time, neither of which is usually necessary in school libraries. The adapted method is described in the *Report of the Secondary School Libraries Committee*.[1] The issue card should be a sizeable one; the report recommends 6 by 4 inches, but this might be inconveniently large for small books. A more generally useful size would be $3\frac{1}{4}$ inches wide by $5\frac{1}{2}$ inches high. A space at the head of the card contains brief details of author and title, also the volume number where applicable, and the classification and accession numbers. The rest of the card is divided into columns for names of borrowers and dates of issue.

The card is kept in a pocket which is pasted on to the inside of the back cover of the book. On taking out a book the borrower extracts the card, signs it, and leaves it on the librarian's desk. The librarian stamps the date on the card and files it either by author or

[1] See Selected References.

classification number; if by classification number this should take precedence of the author's name on the issue card. Filing by date of issue would even be possible if it were wished to enforce a time limit, though it would then be necessary to provide date labels in the books in order to trace the entries on

ISSUE CARD

Brownrigg. 942.07	Home life in Georgian England	vol. 1 (1528)
1935		
A. Martin 3 May √ J. Green 5 Jun. √ C. Edwards 25 Jun. √	B. Williams 28 Jun.	

return. When a book is returned, the librarian finds the card, cancels the date, and replaces the card in the book. This method should be found generally suitable for schools.

Method 3.—This method obviates the necessity for book pockets; all that it requires is a printed slip which is filled in by the borrower on taking out a book. It can be used either as a single- or double-entry system.

The latter is preferable for any library of more than medium size.

A good size for the slip is 4¾ inches wide by 2½ inches, as this will fit easily into a 5-inch tray. The heading "Author's surname" is purposely put at the bottom of the space so that the name when written in comes

BORROWER'S SLIP

AUTHOR'S SURNAME (IN BLOCK LETTERS)	ACCESSION NUMBER
TITLE	VOLUME
DATE BORROWER	

at the top edge. With this method and also with the first method it is necessary to instruct borrowers which is the number required if both classification and accession numbers are given on the book-plate. For making the double record the particulars on the borrower's slip should be copied on a blank slip, or, by the use of carbon paper, borrowers might write a slip and a copy at the same time. If the copying is not done by the librarian himself, the headings of the copied slips should be carefully checked as borrowers frequently give the translator or the editor for the author. It is a valuable form of training to teach pupils to enter book particulars correctly. They should write their entries from the title-page, and where this does not give the necessary information quite clearly it might be a good plan to tip in with paste a model slip in front of the title-page. When a second slip is not used, and when borrowers make their own carbon copies, this precaution will be all the more necessary. The two sets of slips are filed in separate trays. One tray has guide-cards bearing the names of borrowers kept in alphabetical order; the borrowers' slips are put behind these cards. The other tray has guide-cards with the letters of the alphabet and in it the copied slips are arranged in alphabetical order of authors. When only one set of slips is used these will be filed by authors.

When a book is returned, the librarian finds the book slip under the author's name, checks the accession number, and withdraws the slip. The borrower's name on the book slip enables him to withdraw the original slip from the borrowers' file. A count of issues can be made from the withdrawn book slips, and the withdrawn borrowers' slips will give records of the pupils' reading. It is very doubtful, however, if the use made of such a record would be worth the trouble involved, especially as very often teachers like the pupils to keep their own lists of books read. The advantage of the double record is that the personal file is useful for notifying borrowers of any books they may not have returned after a general recall of books and for keeping a check on the number of volumes they borrow. The method is suitable for use when there is no time limit for reading books nor any strict limit on the number of volumes any one person may have. If anyone has out an unreasonable number of books this will be discovered on filing slips for further books taken out and the return of some may be requested. As a check on books retained for an unreasonable length of time the slips might be of three colours, to be used successively for three weeks; then by the time the third colour comes to be used any entries on slips of the first colour would show up as having been out anything from three to six weeks, and steps might be taken accordingly.

FICTION ISSUES

For light fiction and other free-time reading books of which the issues are restricted, a different form of record may be needed. A large-sized card may be used for each borrower with columns for title, date taken out, and date returned; or the book card combined with borrower's card method of charging as used in Public Libraries may be adopted. A description of this will be found in Chapter VIII of a *Manual of Library Routine*,[1] by W. E. Doubleday.

[1] See Selected References.

BOOKS ON RESERVE

A temporary reserve list will help to ensure that all pupils concerned have equal chances of reading books which are for a time in great demand owing to their having been recommended by teachers. Teachers should be asked to notify the librarian of any books they propose to tell their classes to read *before* they actually make the recommendation. The librarian then secures the books and puts them on a special shelf. The best way of distinguishing these books has been found to be by the use of a coloured ticket of thick manila paper which, when slipped into the issue card pocket, projects half an inch above the cover of the book. If there are no pockets for issue cards, they must be supplied for the books put "on reserve." On the projecting portions of the manila ticket the words "ON RESERVE" should be written; the ticket is taken out when a book is restored to its normal place on the shelves. One important library uses a 3-inch band of manila paper, boldly inscribed, wrapped round the cover and folded inside after the manner of the notices of the month's choice of the Book Society.

Books on reserve should remain in the library during school hours and should be replaced by readers on the Reserve Shelf immediately after use. Books "on reserve" may be allowed out overnight, but must be returned before school next day. A special entry book can be kept for these books, or they may be issued only

PORTSMOUTH HIGH SCHOOL FOR GIRLS, SOUTHSEA: THE LIBRARY IN 1934
By courtesy of the Head Mistress

on application to the librarian who makes his own note. A list on the notice-board of all books "on reserve" is useful to readers and serves the librarian as a check list.

BOOKS RECALLED FOR ANOTHER BORROWER

When a book which is in circulation is required by another borrower, application for it should be made by the librarian. The book will then be returned to the library, and can be properly discharged and re-entered to the new borrower; the librarian can also delay making the application if it is considered that the first borrower has not had it for a reasonable period. The entry in the issue register should be marked in some way to indicate for whom the book has been recalled, or it may inadvertently be replaced on the shelves.

END OF TERM RECALL OF BOOKS

A week or ten days before the end of term notice should be given that all books must be returned by a certain date. On the day following the given date some books will be brought back; this may be regarded as a day of grace which the librarian uses to ascertain that none of the books remaining uncancelled in the issue register have been returned direct to the shelves. When satisfied on that point, requests for the return of outstanding books are sent out, with or without intimation that a fine is due according to the library's practice. If a second application has to be made, a fine should certainly be charged, and it may be necessary to mention the amount that will have to be paid for a new copy if the book is not forthcoming. Mention of the price is usually enough to secure the return of a book even when the borrower asserts that every possible place has already been searched. A beat round the shelves and cupboards of the staff room and senior classrooms by the librarian is often productive of sundry missing items. He may also discover that some books have been taken out without having been entered. If the offender can be traced he should be dealt with severely, as taking out books without entering them is an offence that undermines the whole organization of the library.

HOLIDAY BOOKS

Simultaneously with the return of books, lists of those desired for the holidays should be given in. It is most convenient if a standard form is used instead of any odd-sized bits of paper. When there are many requests for certain books, the only satisfactory method is to copy out all entries on to separate slips with name of applicant on each, sort these into alphabetical order by author, and allocate the books as fairly as possible. Books which cannot be supplied must be crossed off the lists and the corresponding slips cancelled. Each person's books are put in a pile with the holiday list projecting so that the name is visible, and the slips are retained by the librarian as the register of holiday books issued.

CHAPTER X

BINDING

It is by no means always easy to decide when to rebind, especially if there is not much money available for the purpose. As a general rule it is fairly safe to say that people who are not acquainted with binders' methods are inclined to leave it too long. A book should be rebound as soon as it begins to be "shaky-loose" in its cover. By binding then the longest life will be ensured for the book. If a book is worth keeping permanently, it is worth making presentable. A certain saving on binding may be effected by proper care of the books; they should not be allowed to fall about on shelves that are only partly full, but should be kept upright by book-supports; above all, shelves should not be crammed too full; this squeezes the sections, and makes it very easy to tear the back in getting a book out. A book should never be pulled out by the top of the back, but just tilted so that the sides can be gripped. When books are received in paper covers, they should be bound before being put into circulation.

In a library that has been newly stocked, only a small amount of rebinding will be needed for the first three years, but afterwards rebinding will become a regular charge if the books are really used. It is fatal to the appearance of the library to let necessary binding fall into arrears. Even if the arrears can be made up, the books by that time will be in such poor condition with the backs of the sections torn and frayed that the binder cannot make a good job of them. Unless there is an unusually good local binder, it is better to send the books to one of the firms who specialize in library binding. If the books are sent off at the end of one term, they should be back in time for the beginning of the next.

INSTRUCTIONS TO BINDER AND CHOICE OF MATERIALS

The list of books sent, together with instructions as to the nature of the work to be done to each book, material, and colour, and date of return, should be sent to the binder under separate cover. A duplicate should be kept for checking the work. To indicate the lettering to be put on the backs of the books, the required words may be lightly underlined in pencil on the title-page. For books of ordinary size, any of the following cloths, which are all fast-finished, are suitable: imperial morocco cloth (this can be had in several grainings), Sundour, and Durabline. Larger books may be bound in buckram, or if they are to have exceptionally hard wear may have a niger morocco back and cloth sides. Any leather that is used should be guaranteed as "Protected and acid-free." The protecting process has recently been discovered after lengthy investigations by leather manufacturers; it arrests decay by preventing the leather from absorbing injurious acids from the atmosphere.

The binder employed should be asked to furnish a pattern book of cloths, and in selecting from these it should be remembered that bright colours are no more expensive than dingy ones. Art shades in leather are to be avoided as they usually fade. Leather backs may be finished with blind-tooled lines, but gold or colour must be used for any tooling on cloth. A point sometimes not realized is that binders charge by the height of a book, so that a thin, tall book will cost more to bind than a short, thick one. If exceptionally thick, or much repairing is required, or a very long title has to be lettered, there will be a slight additional charge.

REPLACEMENT INSTEAD OF REBINDING

It should be borne in mind that there are occasions on which it may be better policy to spend a little more on a new copy rather than to rebind the old. Many standard books, especially on scientific subjects, are almost continually under revision. Old editions of such books are not usually worth spending any money on; they should be replaced by the latest edition. Very often, too, literary texts, especially if relics from some former library and not intrinsically valuable, are better scrapped and replaced by a modern edition such as the "Oxford Poets."

HOME REPAIRS

The extent to which home repairs can be effected will depend on the equipment available. Some schools have a craft shop where pupils are taught binding and allowed to practise on magazines and the less important books from the library. As in all amateur binding, the lettering will be the chief difficulty. This can be met either by lettering with a pen in waterproof indian ink on light-coloured cloth, or by the use of the electric stylus. The electric stylus, which can be obtained from all the principal firms who specialize in library equipment, is a metal point fixed in an insulated holder which has a flex for attachment to an electric light fitting. Good results can be obtained if the lettering is done very slowly and kept straight, but the stylus should be used only by a responsible person who will not touch the point when the current is "on." The writing is done over gold leaf or coloured foil which is burned on to the book where the pen is pressed. The stylus may also be used for putting authors' names on the backs of books which lack this necessary information, or for marking the classification numbers. If such numbers have to be altered, the old numbers can be covered by a neat band of oil paint mixed with best copal varnish.

Under skilled direction quite a number of repairs can be effected satisfactorily, but unauthorized repairs, such as pasting or gumming the back of a cloth book to the sections, should be firmly discouraged. A good deal can be done with very simple apparatus to strengthen pamphlets and magazines. Pamphlets can be stored in filing boxes, but they are more easily found by readers if they are put with the books on the same subject; each pamphlet then needs its own cover. Magazines which are much read soon fall to pieces, and even if the current numbers are put into reading-cases they will not have this protection when they become back numbers.

To make a cover for a single pamphlet two pieces of thin coloured card or heavy manila paper should be cut the width of the pamphlet and slightly longer; this will allow for an equal projection at the corners. A strip of binder's cloth will be required to join the boards, which should be glued or pasted to it about $\frac{3}{8}$ inch apart for a thin pamphlet. The space for a thicker pamphlet can be gauged by fixing the boards in position with wire paper clips and folding the cloth round the back. The original covers of the pamphlet may be detached and the front cover pasted on the outside of the case. If this is done, a compensating piece of paper must be pasted on the inside so as to prevent the board from curling. In order to attach the pamphlet to the case it should be sewn with linen thread to a hinge of a joint-cloth or thin binder's cloth by a pamphlet stitch. This stitch is made by inserting the needle from the inside through the centre of a section in the middle, leaving the end loose inside, then bringing the needle back from the outside about half an inch from the top, then carrying the thread down the centre of the section and bringing the needle out half an inch from the bottom, then bringing it in again through the hole in the middle. The loose ends are placed one on each side of the long stitch and tied firmly over it. If the pamphlet is composed of several sections its hinge should first be pasted to the back to hold it in place. When the paste is dry the hinge should be secured by pamphlet stitches through the first and last sections. The pamphlet is placed inside the cover and the loose flaps of its hinge attached to the cover. A quicker method, and one which will serve for magazines, is to hinge them as above and then paste the original covers one on to each flap of the hinge and a strip of binder's cloth over the back to make it tidy. The advantage of the hinge is that the cover opens easily and does not come away from the back as often happens with covers merely stuck to the back.

Suitable cloths and other materials, also any necessary tools, can be obtained from firms which specialize in educational handicrafts, or from the bookbinder's material dealers whose names will be found under this heading in the Trades section of the Post Office Directory. It is worth while to ask such a dealer if he will cut odd lengths of cloth into rolls of the required width. Cloth, though generally not of such good quality, may also be obtainable locally. A local printer

ST. PAUL'S SCHOOL, WEST KENSINGTON: THE LIBRARY IN 1935
By courtesy of the High Master

or bookbinder would probably be willing to cut a number of boards to one or two standard sizes.

Many books have been written on bookbinding as a school craft, but the methods described are often unnecessarily elaborate for simple repair work. Very useful and practical directions are given in the sixpenny pamphlets on *Bookbinding as a School Subject*,[1] written by Douglas Cockerell for Messrs. G. W. Russell and Son, Ltd., Hitchin, and supplied by them. The first two of the series of five pamphlets will give the librarian all he needs.

Newspapers can be kept tidy by opening at the centre and stitching through the fold with thread; a quicker method which answers quite well is to stab the folded paper with a hand-stapling machine. Four staples put as near the left-hand edge as will catch all the pages are effective and do not interfere with the reader's convenience.

Filing boxes can be made for pamphlets or back numbers of magazines out of three-ply wood with cloth strips joining the edges, the back side being left open. Alternatively, a wide strip of binder's cloth attached to two stout boards which are pierced for ties is a useful way of holding pamphlets together. It is also quite possible to make portfolios on the school premises, though these are more troublesome on account of their size. Transparent holders for valuable prints or for loose illustrations printed on both sides of

[1] See Selected References.

the paper can be made of cellophane, which is obtainable in several thicknesses from British Cellophane Ltd., 179 Tottenham Court Road, London, W.1. The same material might be used instead of glass for framing notices in *passe-partout*.

CHAPTER XI

CO-OPERATION WITHIN THE SCHOOL

THE co-operation of all members of the school can be enlisted by letting them feel that the library belongs to them. They should understand that if they injure or lose books they are damaging their own property, and if they are dilatory in returning books they are depriving others of a fair share in what is also their property. Over and above this care for the common weal in which everyone can participate, there will be many who can render more direct service.

MEMBERS OF STAFF

The members of staff have it in their power to make or mar the part that may be played by the library in the life of the school. Their appreciation of or indifference to the potential assistance and inspiration awaiting them in the library will inevitably be reflected by their pupils. Among the ways in which the staff can contribute to the effectiveness of the library are making themselves acquainted with its resources both for their own use and for communicating to their classes, and taking an active interest in the suggestion and selection of books for addition. A wise selection of books is in itself a guide to reading. More individual direction, specially to students who

CO-OPERATION WITHIN THE SCHOOL 123

are working up subjects for themselves, can and should be given by the staff with the aid of the librarian in tracing sources of information which have been overlooked. Besides the introduction to specific books given by teachers in their capacity as specialists, they may also, when they are form teachers, extend the scope of the library's influence by bringing or sending their form to be initiated into the use of the library (see p. 132).

There are a few small points where failure on the part of members of staff to show consideration may hinder the smooth running of the library. Such are the handing on to pupils of books which they have themselves taken out, the correct procedure being for the teacher to return the books to the library and send the pupils there to make their own entries; failure to notify the librarian previous to making the announcement in class as to books on temporary reserve (see p. 111); lastly, making haphazard recommendations to pupils to read certain books without first ascertaining that these are possessed by the library.

LIBRARY PERIODS

The appreciation of books and literature may be fostered by the allocation of school periods for private reading in the library, with discussion and guidance where necessary. The inclusion of these periods in the time-table can be accomplished only by the co-operation of the staff, for every subject usually wants its full quota. It should, however, be possible to arrive at an arrangement whereby the English Department has a sufficiently generous allowance to spare one period a week, at least for the Middle School, for the purpose. The librarian or a member of the English staff will use the period for occasional readings of poetry and plays and for chats about books on different subjects or books by a selected author. The provision of a discussion room (see p. 26) would make it easy to conduct the periods without disturbing other readers.

SUBSIDIARY LIBRARIES

In schools or colleges where there are libraries subsidiary to the main library, members of staff, aided by such pupils as they may think fit, will generally be responsible for their administration. Libraries of supplementary material on different subjects will be under the specialist concerned, who will select the books and supervise their issue and checking. General responsibility for the co-ordination of subsidiary libraries should rest with the librarian, through whose hands should pass all orders to booksellers and the cataloguing and labelling of the books. Each subsidiary library should be provided with a list of its own books for checking purposes. A combined catalogue on cards of all books in subsidiary libraries, indicating the location of each book, should be kept in the main library. Small collections of books reserved for the use of particular forms or classes are not advised for reasons which are fully set out in Chapter VII of the *Secondary School Libraries Report*.[1] House libraries are usually independent, except in so far as those in charge may like to take advantage of the librarian's experience in the selection of books.

STUDENT HELP

As has been said in Chapter III, it is not necessary that all the pupils who are selected to help in the library should be members of the Library Committee. A sufficient recognition of their services may be conferred by the title of library prefect or assistant librarian. Much good work can be done by these assistants if care is taken to train each successive generation for the office. In order to ensure continuity the assistants should be selected from pupils who have two whole years of school or college before them. During the first year after the introduction of the system all the training will have to be given by the librarian. In subsequent years, the second-year assistants should each be given a first-year assistant to work with him or her and thus learn the routine. Among the various duties which may be undertaken by the assistant librarians are: maintaining correct order on the shelves in different sections and the checking of these at stocktaking time, supervision of the entries of issues, discharging books on return and replacing them on the shelves, notifying borrowers of books to be re-

[1] See Selected References.

turned and collecting fines, putting holiday books ready for issue, effecting repairs to books and mounting illustrations, lettering labels for the shelves and duplicating library notices and forms. Any assistants who show particular aptitude may be promoted to a certain amount of cataloguing, though this should be performed only under the immediate direction of the librarian, and even then will require careful checking to avoid discrepancies.

CHAPTER XII

SUPPLEMENTARY SERVICES

BESIDES the upkeep of the book stock and its administration there are various other services which the library can render.

OBTAINING BOOKS OCCASIONALLY REQUIRED

From time to time works will be asked for which the library does not possess, and which are so expensive or will be so rarely required that, even if still in print, it would not be a good policy to buy them. Under these circumstances, the school librarian will naturally try to obtain the books from another library. The first move would be to apply to the nearest Public Library; if it has not got the book the quest need not end at that, for behind the Public Library are the resources of the regional system of inter-library lending, and behind that again is the National Central Library with its specialist outlier libraries which place their books at its disposal. If one of these cannot produce the book, it must be scarce indeed. It is desirable that school librarians should have a clear understanding of the conditions under which books can be obtained from the Regional and Central lending systems. They are that books must not be asked for direct but through the Public Librarian, who may require the borrower

NORWICH TRAINING COLLEGE: THE LIBRARY
Jarrolds' Photo

to pay the postage. Application should not be made for ordinary text-books nor for any work costing less than eight shillings, unless it is out of print. The book asked for will nearly always be supplied eventually, but when inquiries have to be made in several directions before a copy is located, delays naturally occur. Further details on the system of mutual assistance that is being built up amongst libraries will be found in *Library Co-operation in Great Britain*,[1] by Colonel Luxmoore Newcombe, a book issued in the same series as this.

Schools in London are very fortunate in being able to draw on the Circulating Library for Higher Classes in Secondary Schools maintained by the Council at County Hall, Westminster. In the West Riding of Yorkshire there is a similar circulating library under the charge of the County Librarian. Both these libraries are additional to education libraries for the use of teachers. The school librarian should make it his business to be acquainted with any such means of obtaining the more expensive works in his own area; for instance, most Education Authorities provide some form of lending library for teachers. He should remember also to inquire into the possibility of borrowing or reading privileges being granted by the libraries of the university, if there is one, or of other schools. If the school library, or even any member of the staff, belongs to societies which have their own libraries,

[1] See Selected References.

such as the British Drama League, the Geographical Association, the Historical Association, and the Societies for the Promotion of Hellenic and Roman Studies,[1] books may be obtained from them on payment of postal charges. The League of Nations Union[2] will lend schools up to thirty books for three months on payment of carriage.

INFORMATION ON CAREERS

There is a regularly recurring demand for information on careers, and as much of this is in pamphlet form it is best to provide a special box or file. Loose papers can be kept in it and need not be separately catalogued. The *Choice of Career Series* of pamphlets issued by the Ministry of Labour should be collected; the *Journal of Careers* published monthly by Truman and Knightley is also useful. The Central Employment Bureau for Women[3] issues *Careers and Vocational Training* every three years, and this will be found invaluable by girls' schools. It is very important to provide only reliable and up-to-date information.

DISPLAYS ON CURRENT TOPICS

Attention may be drawn to topics of the moment by displaying on a suitable stand a few books, pamphlets, cuttings, or illustrations bearing on them. An occasion such as the exhibition of "British Art in Industry"

[1] See Address List. [2] Ibid. [3] Ibid.

gives an opportunity to show the illustrated souvenir and some books on industrial art. The topics chosen need not always be of national importance; they may be connected with school activities, such as a lecture by an authority on his subject or an expedition to some place of historical or archaeological interest. There is no need to attempt to keep up an unbroken succession of displays; judicious intervals will make them the more appreciated.

ILLUSTRATION COLLECTION

A very useful adjunct to the book stock is a collection of mounted illustrations and postcards. These can be issued to teachers for handing round in class or showing by epidiascope, and also may be drawn on for displays in the library. Illustrations can be obtained from old magazines, catalogues, withdrawn books, and even book prospectuses. There is a good deal of free material to be obtained on application to railway companies, Dominion Government departments, and so on. For the expenditure of a few shillings, some of the very valuable sets of postcards issued by the British Museum, the Science, Natural History, and Victoria and Albert Museums may be acquired. Some of the bibliographies mentioned in Chapter IV give further suggestions on illustrative material.

The illustrations should be mounted on sheets of fairly stout mounting paper of a neutral but not too dark a colour. In deciding on the size of the mounts, the size of the whole sheet from which they are to be cut should be taken into account so as to avoid waste strips. A good size is 11¾ by 9½ inches, as this will fit into a quarto vertical file. A portfolio may be needed for illustrations too large to go into the file and two or three card-filing drawers, 6 by 4 inches, to take the postcards. When mounting illustrations, they should not be pasted all over, but just touched with the brush at the four corners. Care should be taken to give a sufficiently detailed description of each illustration; a picture of a ship or a chair is not much use unless the period to which it belongs is given.

The illustrations may be classified systematically or arranged alphabetically by subject headings, the arranging number or word being written in such a position that it will show at a top corner when placed in the file. Some tabbed folders will be useful for containing the illustrations on the different subjects. The arranging symbols have to be written on the backs of postcards and their sequence indicated by guide cards.

SCHOOL ARCHIVES

The library is a suitable place in which to assemble reference copies of documents such as the school magazine, prospectuses, programmes, internal examination papers, and any others that may throw light on the history and development of the school.

INSTRUCTION IN THE USE OF BOOKS AND LIBRARIES

The use of the library will be increased if the librarian makes it his business to give help and explanations to readers whenever possible. It is usual to keep a library register which is signed by pupils on admission to the library. The signing of the register gives the librarian an opportunity to explain the arrangement of the books on the shelves, the method of taking out books, and the use of the catalogue. Form teachers should be asked to send pupils in small groups. Before leaving the library, each pupil should be helped to find some book that appeals to him. To let anyone go away empty-handed from a first visit is a great mistake. Actual instruction in the use of books may be approached by a general talk to a group, but as a rule it makes most impression if linked with work the pupil has in hand. Valuable introduction to the use of reference books may be given by compiling a list of problems which can be solved from a few standard works. The questions should be so framed that the answers required are very brief, but such that a pupil could not give from his own knowledge. The list of problems should be duplicated, leaving spaces for the answers. When the pupils selected have assembled in the library, a short talk on the books to be used should be given and then they can begin on the problems. If the same pupils can come several times, the range of problems can be extended and the clues as to where the required information is to be found be made less specific or even omitted. When this stage is reached, the pupils should be required to quote the source they have used, giving author, title, volume, and page references in correct bibliographical form. Specimen forms which have been used for first and second visits are reproduced.

Directed by their teachers, the older pupils may attempt a bibliographical approach to some subject of study. A convenient way in which this may be conducted is for each student to make out a bibliography of books in the library which he thinks will be useful, giving the necessary references in proper form. He also draws up an outline of headings and sub-headings showing how he proposes to treat the subject. The bibliography and scheme of headings are commented on and possibly revised by the teacher. The pupil then uses them as a guide in reading up the subject and finally produces a paper summarizing his findings.

Pupils who are leaving should be given some idea of the wider resources of libraries and the names of some works useful in this connection will be found in the list of selected references. A short talk on municipal and county libraries and their linking up by regional systems and the National Central Library, and on conditions of admission to the larger reference libraries, would be most valuable to those who intend to proceed to more advanced studies.

Date .... Name ....

LIBRARY HUNT I

Find out the following by examining the shelves and using the catalogues. (N.B.—When giving the name of an author, put surname first, then initial.)

1. The classification numbers for
   Birds ....
   Economics ....
   French Revolution ....

2. The surnames of six musical composers whose works are in the Library.
   ....
   ....
   ....

3. How many books by Sir Arthur Eddington there are in the Library. ....

4. The classification numbers of:—
   Lucas, E. V.   A Wanderer in London   ....
   Bulfinch, T.   Golden age of myth and legend ....
   Hugo, V.   L'homme qui rit   ....

5. The average number of volumes in a double-sided case. ....

6. The position of the case which contains the books on astronomy ....

7. How many volumes there are of Bryan's "Dictionary of painters and engravers." ....

8. The author and title of one book entirely devoted to:—
   Lenin ....
   Scipio Africanus............   ....
   Ben Jonson ....

9. The name of a translator of Asser's "Life of King Alfred." ....

10. The names of the authors who have written books on Milan which are in the Library.
    ....

Checked by ....

Date .... Name ....

LIBRARY HUNT II

Find out the following from the Encyclopaedia Britannica, the Dictionary of national biography, Whitaker's almanac, and Who's who. (N.B.—The index to the Encyclopaedia Britannica may be used.)

1. The address of the British Legation in Czechoslovakia.
   ....

2. The day, month, and year of the birth of Archibald Philip Primrose, author of "Napoleon: the last phase."
   ....

3. Where Mr. Montagu Norman was educated.
   ....

4. The length of the river Danube.
   ....

5. The diocese of which Jeremy Taylor was bishop.
   ....

6. The population of Exeter in 1931.   ....

7. The father of Elizabeth Fry.
   ....

8. When the Royal Naval Reserve was founded.   ....

9. The British diplomat who arranged the Treaty of Bucharest in 1812.
   ....

10. The country address of Mr. Baldwin.
    ....

Checked by ....

SELECTED REFERENCES

NOTE.—The prices given have been checked with the latest sources available, though no assurance of their stability can be given. The prices of American publications are necessarily approximate.

Abbreviations: L.A.   Library Association.
              A.L.A. American Library Association.
              (English agents: Woolston Book Co., Ltd., Byard Lane, Nottingham.)

GENERAL

BOARD OF EDUCATION. Memorandum on libraries in state-aided secondary schools in England. 1928. H.M. Stationery Office. 3d.

—— Report of the consultative committee on books in public elementary schools. 1928. H.M. Stationery Office. 1s. 3d.

CARNEGIE UNITED KINGDOM TRUST. [Secondary School Libraries Committee.] Libraries in secondary schools: a report to the Trust. 1936. Carnegie U.K. Trust. A few copies are available on request.

COCKERELL, D. Bookbinding as a school subject: Stage I. Binding books of one section; Stage II. Binding books of more than one section in half canvas. [1930.] G. W. Russell and Son Ltd., Hitchin. 6d. each.

DOUBLEDAY, W. E. A Manual of library routine. 1933. Allen and Unwin and L.A. 10s. 6d. To L.A. members 8s. 9d.

DOUBLEDAY, W. E., *ed.* A Primer of librarianship. 1931. Allen and Unwin and L.A. 7s. 6d. To L.A. members, 6s. 3d.

FARGO, L. F. The Library in the school. 1930. A.L.A. 12s. 6d.

FEGAN, E. S. School libraries: practical hints on management. 1928. Heffer. 3s. 6d.

INCORPORATED ASSOCIATION OF ASSISTANT MASTERS. Memorandum on school libraries. In preparation.

LIBRARY ASSOCIATION. Public and secondary school libraries. 1929. L.A. 1s.

NEWCOMBE, L. Library co-operation in Great Britain. (Practical Library Handbooks.) In prep. Allen and Unwin. 5s.

SAYERS, W. C. BERWICK. A Manual of children's libraries. 1932. Allen and Unwin and L.A. 10s. 6d. To L.A. members, 8s. 9d.

SMITH, R. D. HILTON, *ed*. Library buildings: their heating, lighting and ventilation. 1933. L.A. 4s. 6d. To members 3s.

WILSON, M. School library management. 5th ed. 1931. H. W. Wilson Co. (English agents: W. and R. Holmes, Dunlop Street, Glasgow.) 5s.

CLASSIFICATION

DEWEY, M. Decimal classification. 13th ed. 1933. £2 16s. 6d.

—— Abridged Decimal classification. 4th ed. 1929. 15s. 6d. New edition in preparation.

—— Primer Decimal classification. 1921. 6s. New edition in preparation.
Forest Press, Lake Placid Club, N.Y. (English agents: Library Bureau Ltd., 1 Leadenhall Street, E.C.3.)

How to find a book: a reader's guide to the arrangement of books on the shelves, with an abridged subject index reprinted from the Dewey Decimal classification. Libraco, Ltd., 62 Cannon Street, E.C.4. 3d

LIBRARY ASSOCIATION. Books for youth: a classified and annotated guide ed. by W. C. Berwick Sayers. New ed. [of the work formerly entitled Books to read]. 1936. L.A. 10s. To members, 9s.

138 SCHOOL & COLLEGE LIBRARY PRACTICE

One thousand books for the senior high school library [classified by the Decimal scheme]. 1935. A.L.A. 4s. 6d.

SAVAGE, E. A. A Manual of book classification and display. In prep. Allen and Unwin and L.A. 10s. 6d. To L.A. members, 8s. 9d.

SAYERS, W. C. BERWICK. Introduction to library classification. 4th ed. 1935. Grafton. 10s. 6d.

Cataloguing

AKERS, S. Simple library cataloguing. 1933. A.L.A. 6s.

BRITISH MUSEUM. Rules for compiling the catalogues in the Department of Printed Books. 1927. Oxford University Press. 2s. 6d.

CAMBRIDGE UNIVERSITY LIBRARY. Rules for the catalogues of printed books and music. 1927. Cambridge University Press. 5s.

Cataloguing rules: author and title entries [Anglo-American code]. 1930. L.A. 5s.

CUTTER, C. A. Rules for a dictionary catalogue. Re-issue. 1935. L.A. 5s. To members, 3s. 6d.

LONDON LIBRARY. Subject index. 2 vols. 1909–23. London Library. Vol. 1, out of print. Vol. 2, £1 12s. 6d. to members only.

QUINN, J. H. Library cataloguing. 1913. Truslove and Hanson. 6s.

QUINN, J. H., and ACOMB, H. W. Manual of cataloguing and indexing. 1933. Allen and Unwin and L.A. 10s. 6d. To members, 8s. 9d.

SEARS, M. E., ed. List of subject headings for small libraries. 3rd ed. 1933. 11s. H. W. Wilson Co. (English agents: W. and R. Holmes, Dunlop Street, Glasgow.)

SHARP, H. A. Cataloguing: a textbook for use in libraries. 1935. Grafton. 12s. 6d.

SELECTED REFERENCES

USE OF BOOKS AND LIBRARIES

BAKER, E. A., *ed*. The Uses of libraries. 2nd ed. 1930. University of London Press. 10s. 6d.

BODLEIAN LIBRARY. Readers' manual. 1933. Bodleian. Free on request.

BRITISH MUSEUM. Guide to the use of the reading-room. 1924. British Museum. 6d.

CAMBRIDGE UNIVERSITY LIBRARY. Notes for readers. 1934. Cambridge University Library. 6d.

HEADICAR, B. M. Aids to research. 1931. London School of Economics. 6d.

Libraries, museums and art galleries year-book. Every 2 or 3 years. Simpkin Marshall. £1 5s.

MCCOLVIN, L. How to find out. 1933. Toulmin. 2s. 6d.

—— How to use books. 1933. Toulmin. 2s. 6d.

NATIONAL UNION OF STUDENTS. Guide to library facilities and printed sources of bibliographical information. 1927. National Union of Students. 3d.

NEWCOMBE, L. Library co-operation in Great Britain (Practical Library Handbooks.) In prep. Allen and Unwin. 5s.

—— The University and college libraries of Great Britain and Ireland. 1927. Bumpus. 10s. 6d.

PERIODICAL PUBLICATION

SCHOOL LIBRARY REVIEW. No. 1, April 1936. No. 2 to be issued July 1936. Particulars can be obtained from the Editor: Miss P. de Lépervanche, The Library, Bedford School, Bedford.

ADDRESS LIST OF SOCIETIES AND LIBRARIES

AMERICAN LIBRARY ASSOCIATION,
   520, North Michigan Avenue, Chicago, Illinois.
   (Publications obtainable from Woolston Book Co., Ltd., Byard Lane, Nottingham.)

ASSOCIATION OF WOMEN SCIENCE TEACHERS,
   Hon. Sec.—Miss M. E. Birt, St. Paul's Girls' School, Brook Green, London, W.6.

BRITISH DRAMA LEAGUE,
   9, Fitzroy Square, London, W.1.

CARNEGIE UNITED KINGDOM TRUST, Dunfermline, Fife.

CENTRAL EMPLOYMENT BUREAU FOR WOMEN,
   54, Russell Square, London, W.C.1.

CHILDREN'S BOOK CLUB AND SHOP,
   17, Connaught Street, London, W.2.

ENGLISH ASSOCIATION,
   3, Cromwell Road, London, S.W.7.

GEOGRAPHICAL ASSOCIATION,
   c/o Municipal School of Commerce, Princess Street, Manchester.

HISTORICAL ASSOCIATION,
   22, Russell Square, London, W.C.1.

INCORPORATED ASSOCIATION OF ASSISTANT MASTERS,
   29, Gordon Square, London, W.C.1.

JUNIOR BOOK CLUB, LTD.,
   15, Lower Grosvenor Place, London, S.W.1.

LEAGUE OF NATIONS UNION,
   15, Grosvenor Crescent, London, S.W.1.

ADDRESS LIST OF SOCIETIES AND LIBRARIES

LIBRARY ASSOCIATION,
Chaucer House, Malet Place, London, W.C.1.

LONDON COUNTY COUNCIL EDUCATION LIBRARY,
County Hall, Westminster Bridge, S.W.1.

LONDON LIBRARY,
St. James's Square, London, S.W.1.

NATIONAL BOOK COUNCIL,
3, Henrietta Street, Covent Garden, London, W.C.2.

NATIONAL UNION OF STUDENTS,
3, Endsleigh Street, London, W.C.1.

SCHOOL OF LIBRARIANSHIP,
University College, Gower Street, London, W.C.1.

SCIENCE MASTERS' ASSOCIATION,
Hon. Sec.—The Rev. Canon T. J. Kirkland, The King's School, Ely.

SOCIETIES FOR THE PROMOTION OF HELLENIC AND ROMAN STUDIES,
50, Bedford Square, London, W.C.1.

INDEX

Accession register, 61–63
Accommodation, library, 25–26
Administration, continuity of, 18
Admission to the library, 39
Aids to book selection, 47–49
Alphabetizing, 103
Anglo-American cataloguing code, 93
Annual report, 41
Atlas stand, 33
Author catalogue, 89–98

Bibliographical study, training in, 136
Binding, 37, 114–120
Bindings, strengthened, 55
Board of Education, 20
Bookcases, 29–31
Books—
 addition to stock, 60–67, 70–71
 basic stock, 43–49
 occasionally required, 127–129
 preparation for issue, 66–67
 purchase, 46, 54–56
 replacement, 36, 57, 68, 116
 selection, 37–39, 50–53
 weeding out, 43
 withdrawal, 67–68
Borrowing, regulations for, 40
Budget, annual, 35–37

Card cabinets, 32
Careers, information on, 129
Carnegie Committee, 15, 17, 20, 24, 39, 106, 125

Catalogue—
 alphabetical, 88, 103
 card, 88, 104
 classified, 88
 form of entry, 89–93, 99–100
 rules, 93–98
 sheaf, 104
 temporary, 64, 103–104
 tracing of entries, 103
Cellophane, 121
Chairs, 31
Cheltenham classification scheme—
 outline, 83–85
 suited to schools, 74
Circulating libraries, purchase from, 55
Classification—
 choice of scheme, 73–75
 marks in books, 86–87
 purpose of, 72
Cleaning, 29
Cloth for bookbinding, 119
Committee, school library, 35–42
Co-operation—
 with other libraries, 22–24
 within the school, 122–126
Co-ordinating Committee, 24
County libraries, 22

Desk for librarian, 32
Dewey, Melvil: Decimal classification, 73–83
Discussion room, 26–27, 124
Display rack, 32
Displays on current topics, 129–130

INDEX

Education libraries, 128
Electric stylus, 87, 117
Emergency fund, 36–37
Equipment, 25–33
Expenditure, 35–37

Facsimile bindings, 55
Fiction, issue of, 110
Fiction library, 26
Filing boxes, 120
Finance, 17
Fines, 40, 112
Fittings, 30
Floor covering, 28
Foreign languages, classification of books in, 82
Functions of the library, 16
Furniture, 31

Gangway space, 31
Gifts—
  books, 46, 57
  tables and chairs, 31
Grant, amount of, 17

Heating, 28
Holiday issues, 40, 113
Hours of opening, 39
House libraries, 125

Illustration collection, 130–131
Income—
  allocation, 35–37
  grant, 17
Ink, use of, 41
Ink stains, prevention of, 31
Invoices, checking of, 56
Issue of books, 105–110

Librarian—
  appointment, 18
  training, 20

Library Association, 19–21
Library of Congress classification, 74
Library periods, 123–124
Lighting, 27
London County Council Circulating Library, 128

Magazines, strengthening of, 119
Memoranda on organization, 19
Minutes, 41

National Central Library, 24, 127–128
Newspapers, securing, 120

Office for librarian, 26

Pamphlets, covers for, 118–119
Penalties, 40
Periodicals—
  checking, 57–59
  selection, 36–37
Planning, 25–28
Prices of books, lists of, 49
Public libraries, assistance available at, 22–24

Reading-room, additional, 26
Recall of books, 40, 112–113
Reference books, instruction in use of, 132–135
Regional library systems, 127–128
Regulations, library, 39
Repairs to books, 117–120
Replacements, purchase of, 36, 57, 68, 116
Report, annual, 41
Requisition, books obtained by, 54

Reserve list of books, 111–112
Returned books, 40, 105, 107, 109
Reviews, papers useful for, 49
Rules, library, 39

School archives, 131
School of Librarianship, 20
Scottish Library Association, 20
Secondary School Libraries Committee, 15, 17, 20, 24, 39, 106, 125
Shelf-checking, 68–70
Shelf-list, 64–66, 93
Shelves, guides to, 87
Shelving, 29–31
Silence, maintenance of, 41
Societies, libraries of, 128–129
Societies, subscriptions to, 37
Staff, members of, 122–123
Standing Committee, 24

Stationery, supply of, 35
Statistics, 42, 70
Stock, records of, 61–70
Stocktaking, 68–70
Student help, 35, 125–126
Subject catalogue, 98–102
Subsidiary libraries, 16, 124–125
Suggestion book, 51
Suggestion file, 50–54

Tables, 31
Title entry, 98

University of London School of Librarianship, 20
Use of libraries, instruction in, 132–136

Withdrawal register, 67–68
Workroom, 26

For Product Safety Concerns and Information please contact our EU representative GPSR@taylorandfrancis.com
Taylor & Francis Verlag GmbH, Kaufingerstraße 24, 80331 München, Germany

www.ingramcontent.com/pod-product-compliance
Lightning Source LLC
Chambersburg PA
CBHW061843300426
44115CB00013B/2487